Capitol in Chains

54 Days of the Doghouse Blues

ALSO BY TAMIRA CI THAYNE

Author of

FOSTER DOGGIE INSANITY:
TIPS AND TALES TO KEEP YOUR KOOL
AS A DOGGIE FOSTER PARENT

Editor of

UNCHAIN MY HEART:
DOGS DESERVE BETTER RESCUE STORIES OF
COURAGE, COMPASSION, AND CARING

A DOGGIE HERO IS BORN

Editor and Illustrator of

THE PUPPY WHO LEFT
PUDDLES ON THE FLOOR

Capitol in Chains

54 Days of the Doghouse Blues

Tamira Ci Thayne

EDITED BY JOSEPH HORVATH, M.A.O.M.

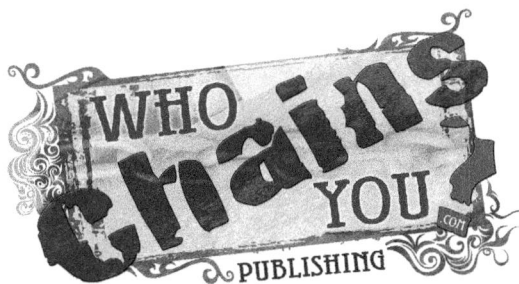

WHO Chains YOU
PUBLISHING

Published by Who Chains You Publishing
P.O. Box 581
Amissville, VA 20106

www.TamiraCiThayne.com
www.WhoChainsYou.com

Cover photo by Joseph Horvath

ISBN: 978-0-6927447-3-4

Printed in the United States of America

Second Edition

~

To Joe
Always Joe, Who Holds my Heart in his Hands.

And All Those Dogs
Still Suffering At the Ends of Chains.
We are NOT Done Here.

Also to those who Supported me
so much during this Chaining:

Joe Horvath

Deb Carr

Mike Romberger

Stacey Romberger

Cathie MacArthur

Melissa Swauger

Darryl Ragastini

Kim Campbell

Deb Warner

Cherie Smith

Justin Strawser

Deb Smith

Amy Worden

Mary Jo McClain

Rayne Brophy

Brynnan Grimes

Ginger Cayo

CPAA

Radisson

Jamba Juice

Gordon Bakalar

Barb & Mark Shaffer

Kel Hatt

Betty Harris

Anna Giza

꒰꒱

Lest it never make it into the annals of history that a woman spent 52 days chained to a doghouse in front of a state Capitol building: I was here.

Preface

Lest it never make it into the annals of history: *I was here.*

Word on the street (in some boring, backwards little town where no one goes and they have nothing better to talk about) is that a woman spent ALL TOO MANY DAYS chained to a doghouse in front of the Pennsylvania state Capitol building hoping to push through a law limiting chaining for Man's Best Friend.

That is correct. And that would be me.

Rumor also has it that I wasn't successful, or as one online commenter put it, I was an "epic fail." True, the law didn't pass. But, I believe there are ways and means of success that are not always readily apparent—actions that push the envelope and have success written all over them even when you can't see it.

In a world evolving (or devolving) into a virtual society, one where we think clicking a button on the internet makes us activists, I hope that reading my story will inspire you to act when you feel helpless.

To stand when your brain screams "fall."

To persevere when every humiliated cell in your body knows you should cut and run....And every yay-hoo with a computer screen agrees.

I am an activist. Come be active with me.

༄

If there's one thing I HATE, it's doing nothing about something.

Introduction
Some Say I'm an Activist; But I'm Not the Only One

ॐ

I was in rescue quite awhile before I learned that 'Animal Activist' was a dirty word. Well, two dirty words, actually.

This baffled me, being a newbie to the world of helping animals, and thinking we were all playing for the same team. I thought being an activist for anything that improved society had to be a good thing. But that's no more true in the world of animal welfare than it is in the world of, well, the animals.

They don't say Dog-Eat-Dog World for nothin', ya' know.

As it turns out, all the animal users and abusers have made the words 'Animal Activist' a synonym for something more along the lines of 'Insane Lunatic.' EVIL Insane Lunatic.

And then, I learned, all the big bureaucratic animal groups said to themselves, "Oh, we don't want to be considered 'Insane Lunatics' so we'd better refer to ourselves as 'Animal Advocates' instead. There, that sounds better."

Then, all the little animal groups—who didn't want to be left out in the Insane Lunatic asylum by themselves—said "Yeah, we're Animal Advocates too. There are no Animal Activists here."

And Tami (that's me), having it in her head that she wanted people to like her, agreed. "Yep, no Animal Activist here. I'm an innocent (e-hem), middled-sized, middle-aged (when did that happen?) woman who just wants to help a couple of doggies. I care about the WELFARE of doggies, that's all. I'm no Animal Activist."

Uh-huh.

At first this felt better. "Aw, see," I thought to myself. "Now I fit in. Now there's nothing for anyone to take offense to, because I'm just a Dog Advocate. It's all good."

But what I'd really done was talk myself into and attempt to render myself small and inoffensive to please others and make them like me.

That doesn't work, because then you don't like yourself.

It was hard to stay small with all the eating I do, and hard to stay inoffensive with all the chainers I deal with.

And even harder to secure the approval of others no matter how small and inoffensive I thought myself to be. The animal welfare types still believed me to be too over the top, and the users and abusers hated me no matter what I did.

So, using the adequate IQ I've touted ever since grade school, I ascertained that something was still amiss with my Be-An-Animal-Advocate plan.

I gradually became annoyed with trying to be something I wasn't.

I'm a LION, dammit! I wanna' ROAR! I'm not a sheep, wandering around bleating and trying to mix in with the herd so I can stay safe!

I wanna ROAR, and, well, ROAR, and whatever else LIONS do, minus the killing of the zebras. I like zebras.

I'm a vegetarian LION, that's all. But I can still ROAR!

What I'm trying to say loud, clear, and proud is: "I AM AN ANIMAL ACTIVIST—YES, THAT'S RIGHT; AN ANIMAL

ACTIVIST."

And turns out I'm not the only one.

Others have figured out the ploy, the divide-and-conquer tactic that is being used by those who want to continue their exploitation, use, and abuse of animals. In convincing animal activists to downplay themselves and their voices for the animals, they weaken the movement and the biggest losers are the animals we seek to release from their human-inflicted hell.

For those of you who see through it and are brave enough to stand tall in your activism, kudos.

For those of you who are just figuring it out, join us. We aren't the only ones.

Some say we are dreamers—but for me, to dream of a day when dogs are recognized as having the RIGHT to a good life inside as part of our pack is not only critical to our success, but crucial for my sanity.

Dream with me.

᎙

To clarify the length of the mission which I called Operation Fido's Freedom:

I (with others) spent every Monday-Friday, 8 a.m. to 6 p.m. from August 2 until October 14, 2010 chained to a doghouse in front of the Pennsylvania State Capitol Building. This totaled 54 days. However, I had to travel for Dogs Deserve Better two of the days for a previously-booked speaking engagement. During these two days (and two other 1/2 days), people took my place and chained in my stead, which I found both touching and brave. You will hear from some of them later in the book. This makes it a bit confusing as to how long I actually spent out there. When I speak of the entire mission, Operation Fido's Freedom, I tend to say 54 days. When I speak of the amount of time I personally spent chained, I tend to say 52 days. I neither want to take away from the time my compatriots spent nor claim the time they spent as my own. I remain eternally grateful to each and every one of them for their courage. Here is a list of the people who chained in my stead when I was traveling:

Deb Smith

Cherie Faus-Smith

Justin Strawser

Ginger Cayo

Deb Warner

Kel Hatt

Betty Harris

Anna Giza

Barb Shaffer

Mike Romberger

Chapter 1
What the HECK Was I Thinkin'?

☙❧

Day One, after my first rain

I know what you're thinking. Wow, that's one crazy beeyotch. You can say it.

My son says it, and I still love him; so as long as you say it with love in your heart, I'll still love you too.

I mean, who in their right mind would stay chained to a dog-house in front of the most important building in the state for ten hours a day, potentially embarrassing herself more than any woman with mental faculties in place in the history of the universe?

I guess me, that's who.

A woman who felt powerless for far too long when it came to getting help for chained dogs, who was tired of feeling that overwhelming sense of hopelessness and loss.

Me, a woman who has fought for chained dogs since 2002, and although she's personally rescued and fostered 180 or more, knows there are far too many dogs spending nights in -2 degree temperatures for her to sleep peacefully.

Me, a woman who has grown tired of lawmakers ignoring our pleas to pass legislation for the past six years and counting, and with no end in sight.

And me, a woman who admired the courage of female activists of yore, those who stood for voting rights for women in front of the nation's Capitol for months on end and even spent time in jail for doing so. Those be some amazing beeyotches! (Said with the utmost love and respect, of course.)

❧

I never cared much for history unless it was brought to life in a movie, then I could get into the story. I got good grades in high school, but when I learned about the suffragist movement—like everything else—I retained it just long enough for the test and then promptly discarded it.

After all, I had lots of partying and boys to occupy my mind and my time.

As I matured, I realized that there may be more to life than partying, making babies, and work. That we may have been put on this planet to evolve and grow, to spend our time wisely instead of frivolously, to leave knowing we did our best, to make a difference, with a conscience relatively-free of regret, guilt, and bad karma.

Not every one believes that, I've realized.

A man I was once interested in, even at the age of 35, still thought we were put on this earth just to procreate. Really? . . . that didn't last long.

☙

In 2004, HBO made a movie about the suffragists called *Iron Jawed Angels*, and area rep Chris Ameduri kept telling me to watch it—but I didn't have HBO on my 20-channel cable plan, so I ignored the suggestion. A few years later I ended up buying the movie when I was in need of inspiration, and promptly became enamored with it.

Not only did it star big names like Hilary Swank, Angelica Huston, and Patrick McDreamy, but the music was so contemporary, the story so compelling, and the women so determined, that I was smitten and watched it every couple of days for weeks.

I wanted to be just like them when I grew up!

I have learned over time and from reading about the greats who came before us, that in every society and in every issue change comes slowly, what is 'right' is not won without a fight, and it usually gets ugly before society's power infrastructure is convinced to make change for the better.

The suffrage movement was no different. The right for women to vote was won only after a long, drawn-out battle which spanned decades, and the women led by Alice Paul and cohorts with the National Women's Party spent many days standing— from sunup to sundown, rain, shine, sleet, or snow—in front of the White House gripping banners that held the president accountable and demanding societal change.

(According to the movie, they even ironed those banners! Now that's fancy.)

Over 200 women were ultimately arrested, imprisoned, underwent hunger strikes, and suffered much brutality before all was said and done and women were finally guaranteed the right to vote by the 19th Amendment in 1920. Wow!

I have a renewed appreciation for my right to visit the voting booth each election day, and a re-affirmed desire to be informed about which reps are animal-friendly so I can make my vote count.

I believe it's my obligation to take voting seriously, because these ladies' blood, sweat, and tears paved my way.

Each time I watched *Iron Jawed Angels*, an excitement bubbled up within me—I wondered how dog activists could do something similar to what these women did for chained dogs. Why couldn't we spend every day on a chain in front of the Capitol in Harrisburg until they decided it might be time for a law? In theory, it was an amazing idea; I wanted to run right out and make it happen.

The idea was intriguing and stirred my blood.

In practice, not nearly so easy or exciting. If only I had twenty dedicated activists, I thought, who didn't have to work and could spend every day chained to a doghouse in front of the Capitol with me...

Ooooh...my dream screeched to a halt.

Who in today's society could spend that much time, would dedicate themselves so fully, could miss that much work and time with family and other obligations?

The wind went out of my sails. The answer flashed over and over in front of my eyes: NO ONE.

Not even me.

But I continued to watch the movie when I felt low or things were going badly with Dogs Deserve Better, and I never failed to get a jolt of inspiration from it, to feel a burning desire to make the same difference these women had.

I watched and dreamed, and tried to figure out how to make it work. I live over 2-1/4 hours from Harrisburg, and had so many obligations at home and for DDB, that I couldn't imagine how I myself could make the time, let alone anyone less on fire for chained dogs than I was.

The dream was on hold.

Months and years flew by, and we had bills limiting how long a dog could spend chained introduced by House Rep Mario Scavello (Republican - Monroe County) and make it to the house Judiciary committee three times in six years.

The first session we never left the Judiciary committee, despite our efforts to rouse the people to e-mail their reps.

The second session (each two years) a lobbyist for the Pennsylvania Legislative Animal Network, Mary Jo McClain, spent a ton of time at the Capitol lobbying the house reps to pass the bill, and was tireless in her commitment to chain-ge.

I was very inspired by her; her efforts, combined with the grassroots campaign, succeeded in getting the bill voted out of committee and onto the floor. A major accomplishment!

Once the bill hit the floor, it was promptly tossed back into the Appropriations committee where it languished until the end of session. No amount of prodding on our parts could dislodge it from this committee.

Heartbreak, again.

✹

Then came the 2009-2010 session, where we understandably expected to make even more progress, hoping our bill would make it all the way to law and finally give some relief to Pennsylvania's dogs and our citizens who tire of seeing this insidious abuse.

Rep Mario Scavello introduced HB1254 early on, and DDB activists were majorly excited to have tethering on the map so soon. Mary Jo was in place lobbying, and grassroots efforts were kicking into gear.

All looked good for a bold and successful campaign!

Then American Humane sent out an e-mail that allowed people to click and send messages to all the members of the Judiciary committee, or maybe it was all the house members, I can't remember. It was so successful that it jammed up the reps e-mail server and mailboxes, apparently infuriating them.

I didn't at the time and still don't see what all the hubbub was about . . . isn't that our job as activists to fill up their mailboxes and not let up until they understand what we want and give it to us?

Yes, I think it is. Of course they didn't and don't like it, but when it keeps happening over and over, sooner or later they will open their eyes and ears, listen to what we have to say, and take action on the bill.

That is our job, after all. To get a bill passed for chained dogs.

It is their job, after all, to listen to their constituents and vote the way the majority of them would want.

So, from what the rumor mill tells me (translation: take this with a grain of salt) Rep. Scavello took a lot of heat from fellow House Reps, and then he sent along that heat to Mary Jo as the lobbyist, and things got ugly from there.

The House bill went nowhere after that.

Mary Jo threw in the towel, DDB brought on a lobbyist who tried to create a more effective grassroots campaign but failed miserably, and the dogs sat in the hot sun wondering why the hell no one gave a shit about them.

Pardon my french.

I was pissed.

To say I was devastated didn't begin to touch the level of frustration and pain I felt at our inability to get help for these dogs.

How long would they have to suffer?

I believed then and still do believe that our personal inadequacies failed these dogs, and that was even harder to swallow than blaming it all on the Reps' failure to act.

If we couldn't get our act together because of human differences and frailties, how could we possibly hope to bring hope to these dogs?

We needed a strong and united front to get through the clutter of bills vying for attention, and we just didn't have it or a clear plan. And we lacked the ability to stir the grassroots enough to flood state reps.

The lobbyist we hired did one great act in that he managed to get a bill sponsored by Senators Alloway and Dinniman into the Senate Agricultural committee, a worthy feat, but it didn't come out until the session was almost over.

Odds were not good that we would have enough time to move it even under the best of circumstances.

It was, again, too little, too late.

✻

I'd been thinking more and more about just chaining myself to a doghouse in front of the Capitol building, without anyone else, because I felt like I couldn't make anyone care about the plight of these dogs, couldn't make them understand how wrong it was from a simple phone conversation or an e-mail, couldn't get through to the powers that be. No one listened.

I felt so powerless and hopeless to help them, that the need to take drastic action just pounded away at me.

Yet the prospect of going and pulling up a doghouse was terrifying too. I would be putting myself in a very vulnerable position, a very public position, and doing something that looked very stupid.

At the most uptight building in the state of Pennsylvania.

I was an introvert—still am, of course. Many people don't believe that about me, but I'm sad to report it's true. I put myself out there for the chained dogs more than I would normally be comfortable with because I feel so passionately about the issue, but a large part of me would like nothing more than to curl up with Joe and be alone for the rest of our lives.

Not only would I have to give up my daily life here with my kids, Joe, and the DDB foster dogs, but I had to give up my own freedom, my ability to go watch a movie when I wanted to, go to the store, do other DDB work, rescue dogs, talk on the phone, exercise, take a nap...you name it, I'd be giving it up.

Would I get arrested when I showed up on the Capitol steps, doghouse in tow? I didn't know.

I found that if I talked to anyone about doing it, they thought I was crazy and always found a reason to tell me I shouldn't do it, to douse the flame of my passion, either through kindness or genuine concern for my welfare.

The lobbyist said I'd kill any chances of us getting a bill passed if I did it, because I'd embarrass the Senators and Reps and piss them off.

Um, we didn't have a chance of getting a bill passed anyway, now did we?

Let's be honest.

So I stopped talking to anyone about it but my nearest and dearest—Joe Horvath, my partner who would support me no matter what decision I made; the DDB treasurer Deb Carr, who'd propped me up more times than I could count; and my best friend Tracy Copes, along with DDB support staff when the time drew closer.

I'd made up my mind: I was going.

Let the chips fall where they may.

Chapter 2
What the Heck Are THEY Thinkin'?

Can you find the dog in this picture?

I know what they're thinking. . . . OK, no, I really don't. And by *they*, I mean the people who chain their dogs for life.

WTH?

I've been working for chained dogs for nine years, and I totally confess that I still don't get it.

People ask me ALL the time, "Why would you get a dog and just chain it outside for life?" ALL THE TIME.

I have no answer for them.

You'd think after nine years I'd have an answer.

Dogs are just like kids: needy and annoying. But you don't chain your kids outside, now do you? (Some of you might want to plead the fifth on that one.)

Did I answer my own question? Do they really chain them because they are needy and annoying? Who knows.

꙳

Do you see the dog in the picture on the previous page? *Can you see him*, amidst all the garbage, old (empty) pans, and other debris?

With no visible food, no potable water? Welcome to the daily world of the Dogs Deserve Better volunteer area rep.

This little guy was rescued in Ohio by DDB Rep Kristin Crankshaw; he was just another piece of the trash, sores all over his body. His before-pictures have stuck to my brain like a bad horror flick.

I want to scream "WHY IS THIS LEGAL? WHY IS THIS LEGAL?!!! [Picture me shaking someone.] WHO CAN ANSWER ME, WHY IS THIS LEGAL??"

I'm a wee bit frustrated.

꙳

I have to admit that dogs really are the neediest creatures on the planet, bar none. My foster dogs are MUCH needier than my kids were on their worst days, except when they were tiny babies, of course.

I've actually had to cage myself IN to my desk area so they stay far enough away (as in one foot) that my computer equipment doesn't get repeatedly thrashed.

Just last week one of my foster dogs got into my area, tangled himself up in the cords, and pulled my laptop to the floor as I raced in from the other room to see what all the hype was about. Luckily neither was the worse for wear.

⚹

When I pull these guys off chains and bring them into my home to foster, they are truly a mess in every sense of the word.

This, to my endless aggravation, is the mess that chainers create when they decide that dogs are needy and annoying, and their poorly-thought out solution is to throw them out on the end of a chain for life.

"Well, that was easy," they think.

But, this should-be-illegal solution only makes them more needy and annoying, not to mention frustrated, territorial, dirty, angry, aggressive, frightened, and frantic. Amongst other things.

And we rescuers are the ones cleaning up the mess.

Or, even worse, NOT cleaning up the mess, but watching a dog suffer in this manner for an entire lifetime, with no recourse to help the dog, no words to comfort the dog, and no one to rely on to bring the dog's torture to an end.

It really has to stop.

I tend to gloss over all the dangers that can befall a dog on a chain, but I realize that's a mistake. I am so indoctrinated in all the dangers of chaining your dog that I erroneously assume everyone knows these dangers, and how they can and will befall an animal left out on a chain for life. Not so.

So let me stop, take a breath, and let you in on some of the dangers of chaining that I personally have seen or read about before we go on.

Dangers that CAN and DO befall chained dogs:

1. Abandonment. The VERY WORST offense, to my mind, because often no one knows that the dog is left on the chain, and without any way to get loose or get help, the dog dies of thirst and starvation. What a horrible, awful, egregious way to die! At least if someone abandons a dog by leaving it stray, it has a chance to find food and water, and a chance to find help and a new, kinder, inside home and family. When chained, a dog has very little chance.

2. Starvation, Thirst. Most chained dogs get too little food and way too little water. At my home, I typically fill my fosters' water dishes 2-3 times a day. How many chained dog caretakers do that? Very few. Typically, if they're lucky, they get water in their bowl once a day, and usually whatever they don't immediately drink is spilled by their chain as they run around frantically looking for love. They are completely dependent on humans to bring them food and water, so if the humans forget or just don't give a crap, the dog goes without. Far too many dogs die of thirst or starve to death at the end of a chain.

3. Physical Problems. A host of physical maladies can be directly attributed to chaining, not the least of which is embedded collars from the chain or collar growing into the dog's neck. This causes excruciating pain as the flesh becomes raw and exposed, or, worst case scenario, the dog dies from his/her neck being literally sawed in half or from infection and maggots which are untreated for so long they cannot be overcome.

Dogs have gotten their legs so caught up in the chain or cable that they have chewed them off to escape, or they suffer nerve or tissue damage from the binding of the cable against the leg or foot.

Flystrike occurs when flies literally eat the top of the dog's ear off. This happens to most, if not all, dogs who spend their life at the end of a chain, helpless victims to fly and other insect bites, including fleas, ticks, and bees. Dogs have been stung to death by hordes of bees descending on them, with no hope of escape or place to hide.

I've taken dogs off chains with all these problems and more. Having rescued my fair share of dogs from chains, I've also seen ear infections, urinary tract infections, rotting teeth, tracheal collapse, blindness, deafness, cancerous tumors, matting, open sores, bloody diarrhea from worm infestations, toenails growing into the foot, etc.

Think about it. If caretakers truly care so little about 'their best friend' that they will leave him/her on a chain for life, how much attention are they paying to physical ailments a dog might have? Virtually none.

Across the board those who chain their dogs will tell you they love them. To that I say BUNK, and that's my kind way of expressing it. There is no truer saying to my mind than "Actions speak louder than words." If you are telling me you love me, but you have no time for me or you abuse me or ignore my needs, you do not love me.

If you tell me you love your dog, but you chain him/her out in the yard and ignore his/her needs, your actions tell me differently. It's really that simple.

4. Predators. When chained, a dog is a sitting duck for any animal or human who comes along to do him harm. The most likely candidates are rabid raccoons, who are not in their right mind and will readily attack anyone or anything they come across. While I was chaining at the Capitol, a rabid raccoon got into my fenced yard and died, with four of my foster dogs having had access to him. Luckily they all had their rabies shots, and none of them appeared to have been bitten, but even so they were still quarantined for 90 days.

How much chance would a chained dog have? Do you know most chained dogs do not have licenses or rabies shots? Well, it makes sense...they are not taken care of, so why would they have the shot that is required by law and could save their life if attacked by a rabid raccoon?

Every winter we hear tales out of Alaska of hungry wolves making dinner out of the Alaskans' chained dogs. I pity the wolves, I know they're just hungry and looking for any food source...but imagine the terror felt by their kin as they are ripped apart by a pack of hungry wolves, no one to protect them, no place to hide.

Of course the worst predator a dog will ever know is man himself. I hear countless stories of the horrors that befall dogs at the hands of man. One that sticks in my mind is of a man in South Carolina who walked up to a dog in a doghouse, tied a cinder block to his head, and set him on fire. Luckily for Pookie's sake, the fire was put out in time to save his life, and the caretaker gave him up because she couldn't afford the vet bills. Pookie, shockingly, made it through and is in a home today. No one knows why the man (predator) did this to him.

In reality, we only hear about a fraction of the wrongs man inflicts on chained dogs. Why? Because they are just pieces of property, and while these owners might be stupid, they aren't stupid enough to leave the evidence of their abuse laying around for others to find. They get rid of the bodies.

5. Temperature Extremes. I hate winter, mostly because the thought of these dogs left out there on chains eats away at my soul. I am tortured enough thinking of ALL of them out there, and knowing that at any given moment, there's probably a dog freezing to death somewhere whose story will never be told and whose life will never be avenged or valued.

But, if there's a chained dog near me that I know about and am unable to help due to our faulty abuse system, I am absolutely wracked with pain and am unable to sleep at night for thinking about his/her suffering.

At the opposite end of the temperature spectrum lies heat exhaustion and certain death from temperatures so high that the dog cannot sustain life and succumbs to what may seem like a sweet relief by then. Dogs do not sweat as we humans do, so panting is all they have to release heat. Without adequate shade and adequate water, a dog faces certain death in the extreme heat of summer.

6. Emotional Distress. Anyone with two brain cells to rub together has to know and understand on some level that dogs are pack animals. But what does this really mean?

Well, in essence it means **THEY DON'T WANT TO LIVE ALONE.** Let me repeat this for any legislators who might be reading this book to see if they are mentioned: **THEY DON'T WANT TO LIVE ALONE!**

Dogs evolved from packs in the wild, and they consider the humans of today their pack, which means they want to live with and be part of our families.

When a wolf or early dog was ostracized from the pack of long ago (or even today), what did that mean to the wolf? An inability to catch prey efficiently, an inability to protect himself efficiently, and, in the end, an almost certain and early death.

It's the same for the chained dog. He or she is banished from the pack, but doesn't know why. Chained by the neck, these dogs cannot move more than a few feet at a time, are nothing more than sitting ducks, and cannot escape any fate that befalls them.

Yet we humans are so disconnected from the needs of the dog that we are perfectly content to sentence our 'companion' to solitary confinement in the backyard with barely a second's thought and wonder what all the hubbub is about when neighbors and animal activists make a stink about it.

The dog, if he has spent enough time with humans to feel this connection, becomes frantic to get back into the pack. So how does she or he express this emotion when a human gets near? Lunging, jumping, barking, and making desperate attempts to somehow connect with the human and let the pack leader know that the dog wants back into the family.

This rarely works, however, and the human just becomes further disgusted at the annoyance of the dog, ignoring him even further and making the dog even more frantic for attention. The vicious cycle continues.

After enough time goes by, and the dog has spent literally every minute of every day watching the door for the humans to come for him, something even more terrifying happens.

He gives up.

A dog who was once frantic and desperate for attention, now—years later—just lays in the mud and ignores his surroundings. He has given up, and is waiting for death to take him. He barely raises his head or wags his tail when the master brings his paltry meal to his dish.

He's emotionally beaten into submission, and the only thing

that will bring him back to being a real dog again is to let him into the pack.

Levi, even when rescuers were there, just looking for his family.

A dog can literally be driven INSANE by living caged or chained, especially if the area is very confined. I've fostered dogs that just walked in circles, and it took months for them to manage the behavior. The worst case I've seen of a dog circling was a foster named Kane, who was some kind of husky mix. He was old and senile, and had spent his entire life on the chain. If we heard him get up in the morning, we had to rush downstairs and put him out before he pooped. If we were too late, he'd just walk in circles in the poop until he made his very own Jackson Pollock painting on my dining room floor. Ick.

7. Aggression. And last but certainly not least, is the rise in aggression in chained dogs. Chained dogs are up to three times more aggressive than your average, everyday house dog.

If you think about it, it makes perfect sense.

What makes a dog aggressive, or the opposite, non-aggressive? There's a bit of genetics to it, as some dogs are born with a greater propensity to become aggressive than other dogs; but most dogs, given the right amount of love and socialization with humans from puppyhood, turn into loving, faithful members of the home and family.

Chained dogs, however, get NONE of these things. They get:
NO SOCIALIZATION.
NO SECURITY, i.e. NO PACK.
NO LOVE.
NO TRAINING.

And people wonder why they attack? Put me in solitary confinement from birth and see if I don't attack the first person who walks through the door.

A dog on a chain is frustrated, angry, and territorial, because the only thing he 'owns' in this world is his little patch of dirt. Not only that, but when someone approaches a chained dog that he or she doesn't know, the option of fleeing has been taken from the dog.

The only choice left is to fight.

The dogs most at risk for increased aggression are: UNNEUTERED - MALE - CHAINED. Guess what? 95% of male dogs that I get off chains are not neutered, so the odds of meeting an aggressive dog on a chain are very high.

Children by nature are innocent and love animals. Children, if not watched every second, are perfectly capable of walking right up to a chained dog. What do you think is likely to happen if this child meets one of the three times more likely to be aggressive dogs?

The child will be bitten, best case scenario. The child will be killed, worst case scenario.

Then, everyone fights about whose fault it was, the parent's or the dog's, and the dog gets euthanized.

Does it really matter whose fault it is? If the dog weren't out on a chain and had been socialized since a puppy, odds are good it wouldn't have happened at all.

If the dog's caretakers are so irresponsible that they think this is the way to keep a dog, do you really think they are watching their three-year-old every minute of the day? Heck, kids even slip away from the most responsible of parents.

Keeping a dog on a chain is tantamount to keeping a loaded gun in your yard and then being upset when your child goes out and shoots himself.

Accidents happen to the best of parents, and children die. But allowing something to continue that increases the child's chances of death or serious injury threefold just blows my mind.

Pennsylvania had a little girl named Brianna Shanor killed by a chained dog attack in January of 2009. She was killed by a chained rottie mix at the home she was temporarily living in while her mother was seeking employment and housing.

It was described, as usual, as a 'freak accident.' Despite attempts to have the media in the area note the link between chaining and aggression in order to educate on the dangers of chaining, the focus was on the dog and not the way he was kept.

I find this so, so frustrating!

We put out a release holding the lawmakers responsible for her death, as we had a bill in play then too; if they had passed the bill and the caretakers complied, her death could have been avoided.

ORGANIZATION CONDEMNS PENNSYLVANIA STATE LEGISLATORS WHO FAILED TO ENACT CHAINING LAW, SAYS "GIRL'S BLOOD IS ON YOUR HANDS"

CALLS FOR IMMEDIATE BAN ON DOG CHAINING IN PENNSYLVANIA AFTER DEATH OF CHILD IN CHAINED-DOG ATTACK

Tipton, PA -- January 26, 2009 -- Tamira Ci Thayne, Founder of Dogs Deserve Better, an organization working to end the chaining of dogs and bring them into the home and family, issued harsh words today for those legislators who blocked a proposed law on dog chaining in the past two sessions: "Her blood is on your hands."

"Her blood" refers to the death of Brianna Shanor, an 8-year-old girl killed in Beaver County by a chained dog on December 19th.

"If state legislators had acted to pass our all-too-reasonable law limiting chaining of dogs for life, there's a good chance that this attack would never have happened. A law which, adequately enforced, would have cut back on chaining, causing most people to either socialize dogs by bringing them into the home and family or at a minimum erect a fencing barrier between the dog and small children, would have and could have saved the life of this child.

Now she is dead, and her mother is forced to mourn her for the rest of her life. There is no easy way to say this: I place the blame for her death at the hands of those in the Pennsylvania House who blocked HB1065 last session. I am calling for an immediate and total ban on dog chaining in the state of Pennsylvania. How many lives must end—both dogs and children—before legislators take the action that is both needed and demanded by our citizens?"

According to an article in the Beaver County Times, Brianna " went near one of several dogs at the property, a more than 100-pound, mixed-breed dog, which was chained outside an old camping trailer that the dog used for shelter. The dog was on a chain 15 to 20 feet long."

A child of Brianna's size and age has no defense against a dog that large—an unsocialized, unneutered, male—bent on attacking and killing.

Dogs Deserve Better has been one of the organizations at the forefront of the push for a state law, and in the last two sessions house bills were put forward to limit chaining. Animal advocacy groups banded together to lobby for the legislation, which last year made it out of the House and to the floor before being blocked and left to die.

Connecticut, California, Nevada and Texas have all enacted legislation limiting chaining, and over 150 cities and counties have followed suit.

For more information on Dogs Deserve Better, visit their website at dogsdeservebetter.org.

Their reaction? Do what they do best...duck and cover, ignore, and bury their heads in the sand.

Unconscionable. Dogs are miserable and aggressive, children are dying, and we continue to pretend nothing is happening?

This is What a Happy Dog Looks Like.

Ezekiel grins from ear to ear.

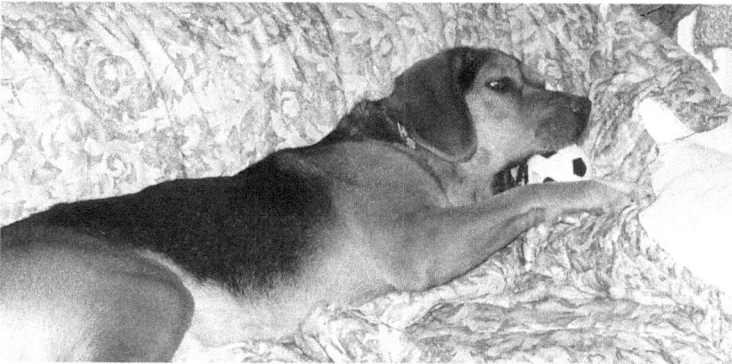

Pete doing something he never go to do before;

lay on the couch and chew a toy.

How Many Happy Dogs

Bear in Ohio, virtually a skeleton on a chain.

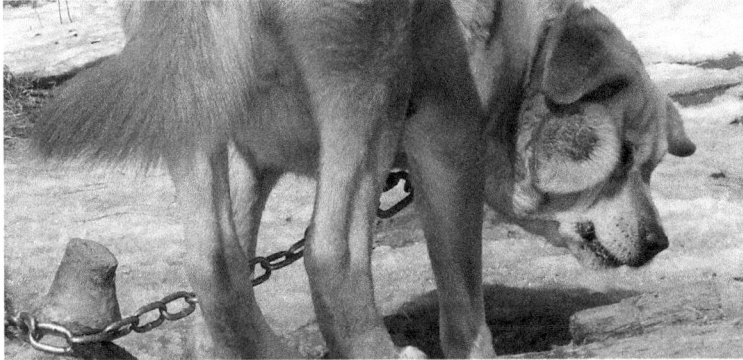

This dog had a huge tumor on his face.

Pete was absolutely terrified of humans.

Do You See Here? I Count ZERO.

Hunter was just another piece of the garbage.

Bunny's entire pen was filled with feces.

This husky destroyed her doghouse out of boredom and frustration.

Chapter 3
Our Reps LOVE Their Dogs...Don't They?

See, I'm bigger than the Capitol Building!

Most any State Rep or Senator will tell you they LOVE their dog. They will get out a picture of their dog, tell you what breed he/she is, and tell you how their dog sleeps with them every night. (Well, except for a couple who happen to CHAIN their dogs, scarily enough; how do these people get elected? Oh, that's right, never mind.)

What they won't tell you is that they know the chaining bill is important and they are planning to vote for it.

What they won't tell you is that they somehow see a difference between the needs of their own dog and the needs of the dog of the very same breed, sex, and hair color that is sitting on a chain at this very moment wondering when or if someone will ever come for her.

I don't get that.

For instance, my own Senator, John Eichelberger, has two Airedales, and is married to a local newscaster in my area. I know these dogs live in their home with them and are well-taken care of, and the couple supports Airedale rescue.

But, he voted against the puppymill legislation that was passed in 2008, even though there's an Airedale puppymill right in Blair County. I've been to this puppymill to pick up a dog they dumped onto Airedale rescue, and the dog stunk to high heaven, had no manners, and was a matted mess. These people don't take anyone into their barn to see how the dogs are living, but I'm sure I can guess as well as you can.

I don't get the disconnect.

When did dogs become a cash crop?

How can you look your dog in the face each night and tell him you did nothing to save his kin?

Does he really believe dogs are just a piece of property when he shares his life with dogs, gets to know what they like and dislike, sees their absolute adoration of him in all his human frailty, knows they have emotions and needs and wants, understands they are pack animals and as such do not live well alone, especially when they are tied by the neck like they are just an inanimate object kept from going adrift?

Does he?

[Don't worry if I'm pissing him off here. I think I already done did that. But I'm speaking on behalf of his dogs, too...John? Your dogs told me to tell you to vote for anti-chaining legislation. Thank you.]

When I got my blow-off e-mail from him saying he wouldn't sponsor HB1435 but he would 'look at it' when it hit the Senate floor, I sent him back a picture of this Bellwood Airedale on a chain and told him that there were plenty more just like this one waiting for his help and not getting it.

No further response from him, but I can tell you he never stopped by to see his constituent [me] when I was there on a chain advocating for these dogs, and he had no time to meet with me at this year's lobby day.

Don't get me wrong; thankfully, some of our reps and senators do get it. And they are co-sponsoring our bill and voting for it when they get a chance; yet most have not yet had the balls to really get out there and go to bat for the bill and push for it to move to the floor.

Wake up, ladies and gents! Your dogs sent me. Do the right thing.

Thank you.

Chapter 4
The Chained Dog Blog

☙❧

You know it looks like fun!

So I packed up my doghouse, and I went to sit in front of the Harrisburg State Capitol Building for 52 days.

The End.

No, really, I have a secret to tell you. It wasn't fun, at all. Well, at least not 99% of the time.

But I went, I committed to it, and I wrote a daily blog, which follows amidst photos stashed here and there for visual stimulation. Check out the skinny on how it went down...

My chains piled on the back deck chair in anticipation of our mission.

A Law Against Chaining

OPERATION
PASS TETHERING LEGISLATION FOR CHAINED DOGS
FIDO'S FREEDOM
FIDOSFREEDOM.COM

Brianna Shanor, 8, died of a chained dog attack in 2009, even after 4 years of legislative efforts. Still, the legislature has failed to pass a law protecting children and dogs.

Would have Saved Brianna. Pass SB1435

This sign was affixed to one side of the doghouse to highlight the danger that chaining our dogs for life poses to children.

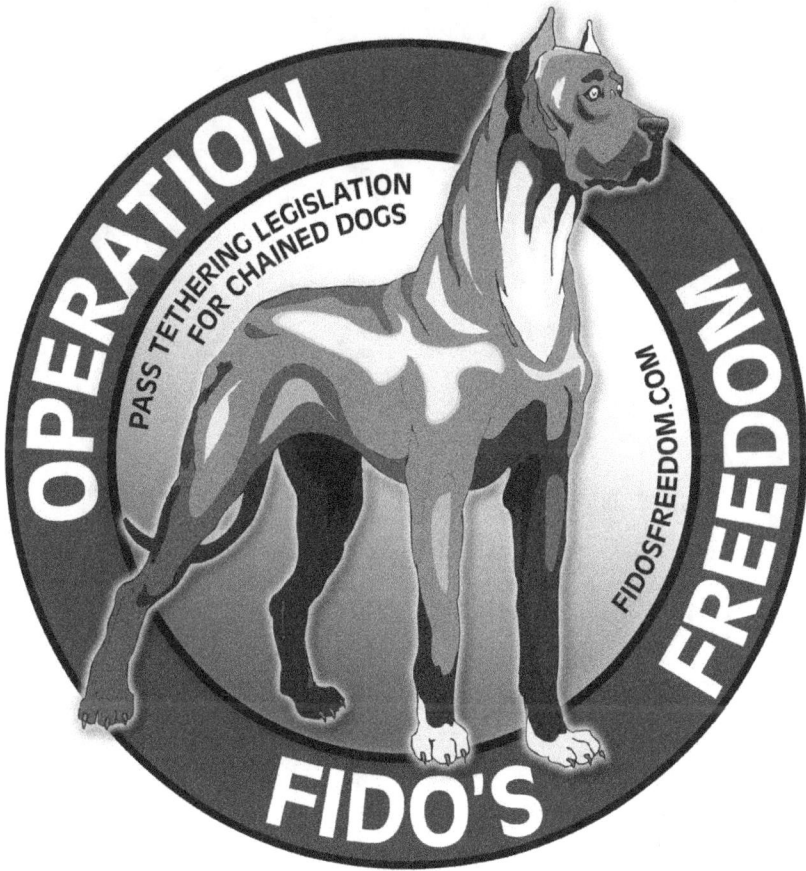

I came up with the name Operation Fido's Freedom for the campaign because I thought it'd be cool with my military background. I used the Pennsylvania dog, the Great Dane, totally by accident—I liked how this dog was standing so strong, fearless, and capable. Apparently William Penn had a Great Dane, hence the PA dog. Who knew. From the Symbols of the US website: "The Great Dane was designated the official state dog of Pennsylvania in 1965. A portrait of William Penn and his Great Dane hangs in the Governor's reception room. . . . PA Legislation states that naming an official dog of the Commonwealth would 'recognize the steadfast service and loyal devotion of all dogs in Pennsylvania.'" *Interesting that PA can acknowledge the loyalty of our dogs. I wonder, have we proven ourselves as loyal to them as they have to us? I think not.*

Have we proven ourselves as loyal to our dogs as they have to us?
I think not.

Pre-Day 1
"I'm here for their law. The chained dogs."
Open letter to PA State Senators and House Reps.

August 1, 2010

୬ଓ

"The world is a dangerous place, not because of those who do evil, but because of those who look on and do nothing."—Albert Einstein

Knock, knock. I'm here for the law for the chained dogs? You've probably just been busy. I know how that goes, I've been busy too. But thing is, here we are almost at the end of another legislative session, and the dogs still have no law to protect them.

It's not right.

So I've come to remind you.

I'm here for their law.

I intend to stay awhile, and I'm hoping that, together, we can get this thing done. Time is short, and they've suffered enough.

Yeah, I know I should be doing other things. A million other things, like having a life, working on other Dogs Deserve Better campaigns. Rescuing chained dogs, one at a time, from those few who see the light or want a convenient place to dump their garbage. Even spending time with my family would be nice. Dinner for Schmucks just came out this week—it looks really funny—and the Carmike Theatre near my house has $1.00 sodas on Tuesday.

But, I can't get away from the nagging thought that they've still got nothing. We've waited six years for a law for them. Through HB1911, HB1065, HB1254, the Casorio/Caltigirone bill we were promised but never materialized, and now SB1435. It's been exhausting!

And yet, here we are still without a tool to help them, and they are still suffering. Many waited their entire lives for help that never came, and have now turned to dust, never knowing a kind word or the kiss of love.

Maybe it doesn't matter to you, but it matters to me, it matters to the majority of Pennsylvania dog lovers, and most importantly, it matters to them.

Have I mentioned yet how the chained dogs are suffering? As they suffer, I have decided to bring their suffering to you, because maybe you have just been too busy to notice. I'm sure if you did notice it, did comprehend the pain of living as they live day in and day out, you'd have taken the necessary action to end it by now.

As they remain shackled to one grassless spot 24 hours each day, I will stay chained in front of OUR Capitol (I think the Capitol belongs to all Pennsylvanians) for ten hours Monday-Friday, 8 a.m. to 6 p.m. As they go without food and water, so will I fast each day from Monday through Friday. And as they are subjected to the elements, so will I be drenched when it rains, wilt in the summer heat, and shiver in the cold of approaching winter.

So that you may begin to really UNDERSTAND their suffering, I am bringing it to you. Let's get this thing done. I'm here for their law. —Tamira Ci Thayne, founder and CEO, Dogs Deserve Better

P.S. If you're looking for me, I'm the woman chained to the doghouse in front of the Capitol.

The doghouse being prepped on my back porch.

Dogs are like kids: needy and annoying.
But we don't throw our kids out on a chain, now do we?
(Don't answer that.)

Day 1
Whew. Glad I Don't Have to Do THAT Again.
Oh, Wait...

August 2

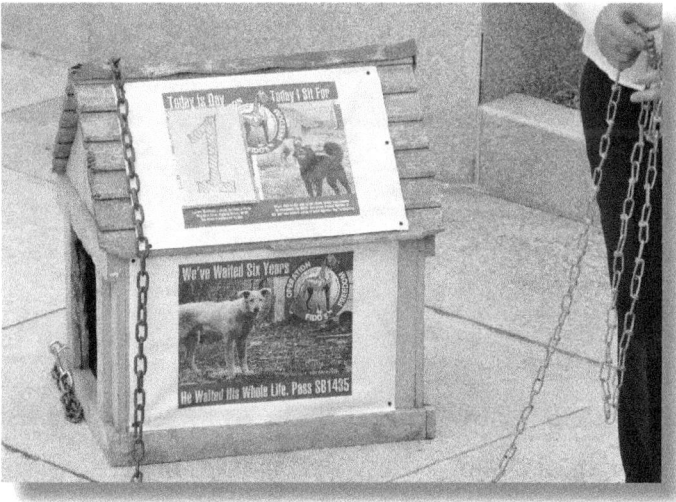

Note the -1- standing for Day One. Oi, it's gonna' be a long siege!

Seems like I just got off a chain. Chain Off (our annual campaign where activists chain themselves to doghouses to raise awareness around the 4th of July) took place a month ago—guess that 24-hour stint on a chain stuck in my mind.

Well, we all know why I'm here, if you read my Open Letter to PA State Senators and House Reps...and you all know what I want. You want it too, right?

A big reason for me to be here is to inspire YOU to take action on behalf of chained dogs…so please, please, please contact your reps, and contact them again; don't stop. They come back to session in September, so if we all pitch in to let them know the time for rhetoric and empty promises is done, we can get them ready to take action by then.

First things first, though; let me just tell you that I made it eleven hours without peeing! I know, that's personal information that you were really happier not knowing, but how can I not share a personal record like that? If you knew me, you'd indeed know how much of a miracle that really is!

Granted, it's probably not a good thing for my kidneys and bladder. But still, there it is. Now you know.

OK, whose pea-brained idea it was for me to fast for the dogs who are starving on a chain with no way to get food for themselves? I know it was mine, but still...now I'm starving (yes, I know I have a buffer that the chained dogs don't) too and I don't like it. Not one bit.

I'm on the record as against keeping up the not-peeing thing, which is problematic given that I shouldn't abandon my stuff for the time it takes to tinkle, and can't see myself dragging a doghouse and chain into the nearest bathroom.

The dogs have it made over me in that area, what with their ability to squat wherever and whenever they please...as long as it's within the ten square feet of their doghouse, of course.

Right across the street from my doghouse (hey, maybe I could get an address for my house? Like on Harry Potter... Tamira Thayne, the Doghouse at the Foot of the Capitol Steps, Harrisburg, PA) there's two establishments, the Caffeine Connection and Sammy's Authentic Italian Restaurant. Maybe one or both of them will give me bathroom privileges in exchange for mentioning them in my blog? Which won't be hard to do, given that I'm dying of thirst and starving to death, and I stare longingly and with drool hanging down my chin across the street wishing I were in there eating and drinking with my friends too.

I hope I don't get a bladder infection. I got this dog off a chain once who was peeing blood in the snow. The vet said he'd just gone too long without enough water and it messed him up pretty bad. He was one of the lucky ones who got off the chain, into rescue, and into a home where he was able to know love and live as part of the pack. One of the very few.

Do you know what happens when you call the humane officer about the rest? Nothing. As there's no law against it, you're lucky if the officer even attempts to educate the caretakers that there are better ways. Most of the time they tell the people they are fine, and you are the bad guy for reporting it.

Don't believe me? Give it a go. Try to get help for a chained dog...let me know what happens.

These dogs NEED and DESERVE a law. Period.

Each day I will sit for different dogs, different breeds we've photographed, dogs in different Pennsylvania counties, etc. Today I start off for all those that have died on the end of a chain; the ones that got old, and then sadly disappeared from this earth. They never got the chance to know love, never knew laughter or hugs or a family to call their own. Rest in peace babies, we're fighting for you. We won't give up until others are guaranteed a better fate than you had.

Observations from today's chaining:

1. I sat down at numerous times on the oh-so-hard granite wall, but I'm confessing because it felt like cheating. I don't think I can stop. My feet hurt too bad, and I can only pace for so long.

2. People were taking their lunchtime walks, going to Sammy's for a meal with co-workers, and just taking their freedom for granted. Chained dogs deserve this too.

3. I didn't explain this right in my 140 character tweet, so I have to try again. Three foreign older people came up to me and asked me in a heavy accent if I had quarters for parking. I said "No, I'm chained to this doghouse." They wanted to know why, so I explained. The woman agreed with me, and took a flyer. Then she said, "It would be better if you had coins too."

4. Note to self. Wearing white shirts in the rain is bad policy. Granted, Weatherbug said only a 30% chance of rain today, but obviously the Bug was wrong. Plus, the chain kept unbuttoning my shirt. Embarrassing! And, it was ruined by the rust. White is out.

5. REALLY not looking forward to that all day rain. I couldn't sit down at all when it rained, so I had to pace the whole time, and I think it rained for half an hour...what am I going to do in the all day rain?

6. Joe came up and took pics for me, and I just wondered if I ever mentioned how much I love that man?

I'm SO glad I don't have to go back tomorrow...oh, crap, wait!

Day 2
My Mission, Should I Choose to Accept It

August 3

☯☯

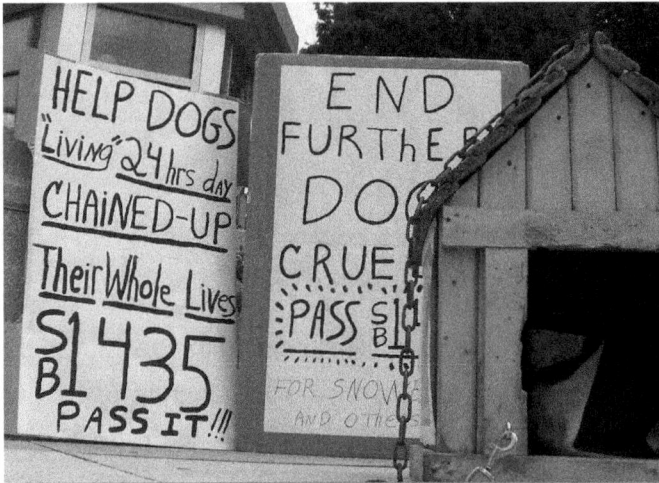

My new friend Darryl's signs picked up business.

Long before I started Dogs Deserve Better, I was on a mission to discover my mission. I knew I didn't want to die without making a difference, and judging by the nasty comments on the article posted in Penn Live today, I guess it's working.

I'm annoying the hell out of those people who's mission it is to criticize anyone with a mission.

Pretty crappy mission, if you ask me, but they're the ones

who have to look themselves in the mirror every morning and say, "Well, who shall we abuse today?"

I spent a lot of time in the self-help book section attempting to point my life in a positive direction. Every time I would ask God what my mission was, a picture of the dog up the road would come into my mind, just like one of those little thought bubbles. I would shake my head and say, "Oh, no, God, that one's too hard. I'm gonna' need an easier one."

The dog up the road, Worthless (yes, that truly was his name), was a black lab mix with a stumpy tail, and a sweet as sugar disposition. I loved him dearly, but there he was, chained to a post in the yard, always tangled around a tree. I used to sneak up and give him food and water, until they told me to stop.

For two years I watched him suffer and grow old, until I finally could bear it no more.

I accepted my mission.

After today's chaining, I'm thinking about that old me who just knew chaining was too hard of a mission…and I'm inclined to agree with her.

What was I thinking committing to doing this every Monday through Friday? Not eating? Working late each night to catch up on the work I missed while I spent ten hours chained to a doghouse? Nursing sunburn, aching bones, stinky feet?

Reporters began to take notice of the chained lady...at least for a day or two.

I am thinking that YES, it IS a very hard path to tread, but that's exactly why I'm here. If it were easy to live chained to a doghouse, for dogs OR for me, I wouldn't be here. But it's not easy.

It SUCKS.

And I know all the naysayers and nasty-grammers will say "people aren't dogs." OK, that's the one thing you've got right. People AREN'T dogs, people are MUCH more capable of living by themselves than dogs are.

People don't need people the way dogs need people. Dogs are the neediest creatures on the planet, bar none, and to chain them up like their social nature doesn't matter is just beyond insensitive...it's genuinely moronic.

One passerby touched my heart today. He was a big, strong-looking guy from Juniata County with a short, marine-style hair-cut. He told me he hates seeing chained dogs, and every time he drives by this one mangy dog near him who spends his life chained, he feels so much empathy for the dog he wants to cry. He tears up as he's telling me about it even.

This is one aspect of the whole need for a chaining law that legislators don't get…not only are the dogs suffering, but those of us who have to watch them suffer are tortured right along with them.

Why should we have to be in constant pain because you can legally torture your dogs? No, not acceptable.

Today I sat for the dogs in Mifflin County. May you know your voices were heard, more so than ever before. In fact, you were part of a media frenzy, I believe I gave eight interviews today!

Wave as you drive by the Capitol in the next few weeks, you know my address: the Doghouse at the bottom of the Capitol steps, Harrisburg, PA.

Observations from today's chaining:

1. People here are still giving me funny looks, but the natives are starting to accept me. This would be a time that being ex-

troverted would help, but I look at them warily, as a chained dog who's been beaten and doesn't know if she can trust again.

2. The weather wasn't too bad today, although I still got a little sunburned. Unfortunately the next two days are supposed to be much hotter AND have a 50% chance of showers. Sweet!

3. A few people from the Capitol started to come out and tell me "We heard you were here." Can you imagine that water cooler conversation?

4. My new computer programmer friend made signs for us. They helped draw people in, which was cool. But, then they kept blowing over, and I felt annoyed that I had to put them back up. *Like I had anything better to do?*

5. LOVED the Channel 8 guys, they spent over an hour video-taping and asking really insightful questions. [I never did see this interview, darnit.]

7. Two guys in a pickup truck drove by and shouted "You're the only one protesting." At least they can count to one. Probably have a chained dog at home.

Talking to a reporter, DDB Treasurer Deb Carr seen in the background.

Day 3
Now I've Gone and Done It

August 4

ॐ

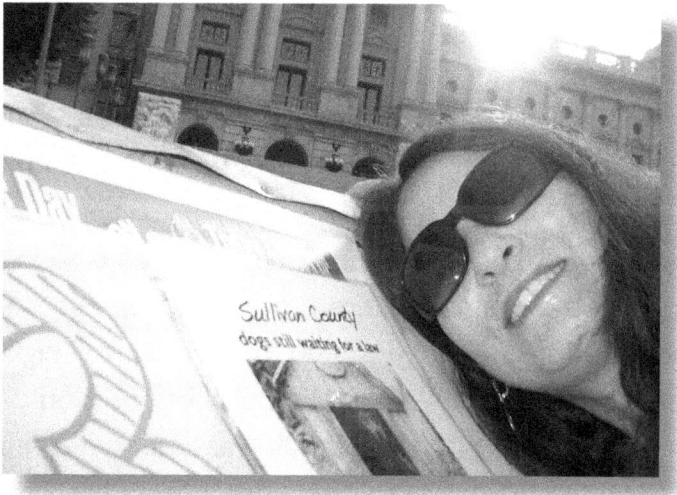

Taking my own photo, isn't as easy as the teens make it out to be.

I swore I wouldn't keep talking to you about pee. I mean, who the heck wants to know about something like that? But darned if I didn't go and get a UTI (urinary tract infection) from Monday's bright idea of not drinking or going potty all day. (I know, I can hear you all say "I-told-you-so" in the background.)

I told Joe, my beau, that I suspected a UTI, and he asked me when I proposed to go to the doctor. I said, innocently,

"Saturday?"

I can't miss 'work' tomorrow! I just got there this week, what would the neighbors think if I didn't show up to work my corner of the Capitol?

He wasn't overly fond of that idea, so after a little internet research, I decided it would be best to seek out a local VA. I depend on them for my healthcare, and I refuse to say a bad word about them because I'm grateful to have a place to go for medical care.

So I called a nurse on duty, and she told me I needed to seek treatment within the next twelve hours. Damn. This didn't fit really well with my plan of working until 11, blogging about the day and trying to catch up on the e-mails that are laying around. But, I realized that going now before it got too bad just might save me a world of hurtin' come this weekend. And I can't be sick this weekend!

I have eatin' to do! And boyfriendin'! I can't be lollygagging around at some hospital where I might not even get food, and I only get to eat from Friday at 6:00 through Sunday night!

So, reluctantly, off I went to the Lebanon VA Medical Center, which was about 40 minutes away. It was actually VA record time (I swore I wouldn't complain) and I was out of there and back at my hotel by 10:15. The diagnosis was UTI, but the culture won't be back for two days, at which time I'll find out if they gave me the right medicine.

Seems that I ended up like Aldus (the dog in Day One's blog) after all. Peeing blood and in need of immediate vet care. (Get it, vet…he needed a vet, I'm a veteran…it was a play on words. Oh, never mind.)

Let this be a lesson to all of you. Next time you chain yourself to a doghouse and think you can emulate the dogs by going all day without drinking and get away with it, think again.

Some items of note from Wednesday's chaining:

1. Wheatgrass rocks! I never had it before, but Steve from Juicy Rumors gave me a shot of it. I was taking little sips and he said you usually just slam it down. I told him, "Yeah, but I'm not eating, so I have to savor every flavor, even if it's grass."

2. Did three interviews today, one with Altoona news station over the phone, and two with radio stations. Kinda' surprised by that, figured I'd done them all yesterday. You don't see me complaining. I want to get people fired up for this law!

3. The heat index hit over 100 today. When I got in my van, it said 95 in the shade. It was a hell of a day. I was pretty much covered in sweat from 8-6. At about 3 p.m. the State Street Building across the street blocks out the sun. I looked forward to that time.

4. I got as smart as a chained dog and when the shadow was about to hit my area, I drug my chain over and got in early. I've seen chained dogs seek out the tiniest bit of shade and try to stay in it. Pitiful, really. Now I totally get it.

5. I think I left all the salt in my body on the Capitol steps. I wonder if they'll make me come clean it up?

6. Had a fair amount of company today, starting with Morgan, Steve from Juicy Rumors' 14-year-old daughter, who loves to come over and be an activist if she agrees with whatever is being

activated upon at the Capitol. She's adorable, and reading the Warriors book series, which is what my daughter and I read too. She couldn't wait to take my place on the chain for the potty break!

One of our DDB supporters was telling me she got a dog off a chain not too long ago. She had watched this dog for a couple of years, and it really ate away at her. She found out the lady was moving, so she got her phone number and asked her if she could have the dog. Now she lives with them, gets to run in a two acre fenced yard, play with her doggie siblings, and sleep in the house with her pack. Awesome!

7. Got the nicest text from my older brother Lance! My family isn't close, so this text really touched me: "Hey, Tam, I saw your newsletter and Vince also sent me an article about you chaining yourself in front of the state Capitol. I want you to know how proud I am of you, how touched I am by what you're doing, and at the same time angry at the gutless politicians who are afraid of losing just a few votes rather than doing the right thing. I love you, Sis, and I think you are an amazing lady!" Wow!

8. Now, call me crazy, but I really think if you fast for three days you should lose like 30 pounds. I'm pretty sure I suffered at least 30 pounds worth!

9. When I got to my spot this morning, there was a reporter in my 'territory' and not there to interview me. I must have forgotten to mark it last night. Luckily one of my foster dogs that I got off a chain four years ago came to visit me, and I encouraged him to mark the territory for tomorrow. Hopefully no one will encroach again, or I'll have to bite them.

Oh, crap, I DO have to go back again, mommy?

Dogs Deserve SO much Better! [And so does Tami.]

Day 4
Dichotomy in Tami-Treatment Highlights Americans' Apathy about Animal Abuse

August 5

☾☾

People love to pretend I don't exist sitting here.

I'm not gonna lie. Today was tough, but not weather-wise as expected (was supposed to be heat index of 104 degrees plus severe thundershowers and didn't happen). It was because I let the naysayers and critics get me down.

I know logically they're there and I need to just go about my business and ignore them, but today it wasn't so easy in practice.

I think of the amazing soul of Nelson Mandela, and how he suffered, and it gives me strength to stop whining and just get on with it.

I did almost cry today, more than once, but the peach incident was what really laid me low. The peach lady drove up, parked her blue pickup truck full of peaches right in front of me, got out all bubbly wubbly, and waved to her three friends who were obviously Capitol employees and were walking down the steps toward her.

The three women passed me closely without looking at me or even acknowledging my presence, and she started telling them the three kinds of peaches she had, which I assumed she was selling.

But, turns out she was giving them to these women. They excitedly oohed and ahhed, took their bags of free peaches, and pranced right past my doghouse again, never saying hi, and certainly never offering me one of their free peaches.

The extreme indifference to suffering or lack of plain old human kindness displayed by these women really knocked me for a loop. I could probably die chained to this doghouse and no one from the Capitol would even notice until I started stinking three days later as they stepped over my rotting body.

It's exactly like the chained-dog caretaker in North Carolina who, when Animal Control told her the dog was dead, said "Why didn't anyone tell me?" The dog laid there for days, dead from starvation, and she didn't even notice? How can you not notice a dead dog in your backyard?

The fact that I am well-dressed, a veteran, hold a master's degree, have written one book and edited another, and am founder of a nonprofit means nothing to them. They don't know and they don't care. They don't see me at all.

As I was really grappling with the turmoil of that experience, Stacey Romberger and two of her office mates came walking toward me with big smiles on their faces, and Stacey was bringing water. For me!

My friend Gordon Bakalar brought a cooler with ice and water and chained for me during a potty break; Deb Smith and Barb Hacker both stopped by with water, while Melissa Swauger and Darryl came by with Gatorade. Sandra Stegman brought me grapes which I'm saving for tomorrow night, and another unknown woman came with water as well.

I've got enough liquid for tomorrow already!

I shared a water with one of the local residents who is down on his luck, and he in turn shared his Mayan wisdom with me. He told me that no matter how people treat you, you hold true to your belief and your passion, and you cling to that, you never let it go. He took the time to minister to me spiritually even in the midst of his own personal crisis.

It's obvious to me there are people who think about the suffering of others, and reach out to help whenever they can. And there are people who turn a blind eye and walk right on by.

But I'm here, and I intend to stay, through good days and bad. I committed to these dogs, and when I am pacing, dragging my chain, just about out of my mind with boredom, I look down at the picture of the day, and I see these faces looking toward me with hope. I cannot let them down.

Miscellaneous observations from the day:

1. Thank Dog for 100 SPF sunblock. I'd be crispy crittered without it.

2. I deserve the best in life, just as the dogs do. Both the dogs

and I (and YOU) deserve a loving family, freedom to choose, access to good food and water, a decent living environment, to be seen, to be clean and have shiny fur/hair, to play.

3. People really do think it's ok to attack other people just because.

4. I need to get a tougher skin. Maybe all the sun will help.

5. A musician named Gravy came up and entertained Sandra and I with three songs. She came to play for 'the dog lady.' She was so good we got goose bumps!

6. Only 24 hours until I can eat. I just can't wait!

7. Mike Romberger's arranging someone to be there every night at 6:00 to help me get stuff into the van. How sweet is that?

Day 5
This is What a Law Does

August 6

☉☉

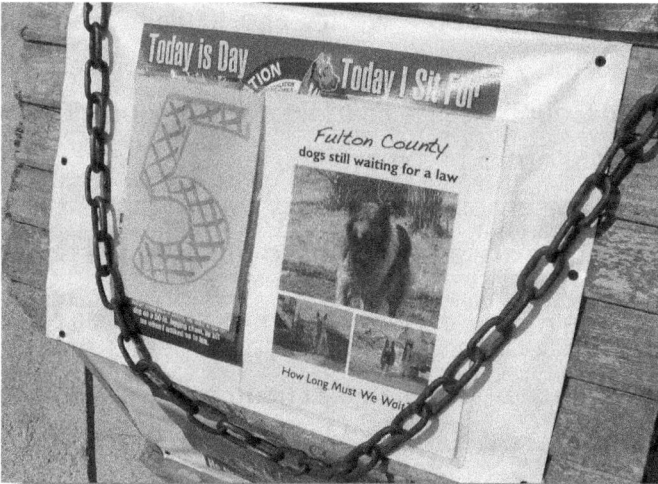

Day 5, Sitting for the dogs of Fulton County

Aproposed Toledo dog chaining law would include "a 15-minute limit for chaining a dog outside unsupervised and prohibiting chaining a dog within 500 feet of a school."

I love the 15-minute limit unsupervised! Presumably it's longer supervised, which I can understand and live with, but by stating this and also putting it into context of the proximity to the school, they are recognizing the fact that chained dogs can and do become more aggressive than other dogs, and are seeing it as a measure to protect their children too, as a community solution, and not just a--gasp--'animal rights' solution.

In West Palm Beach, Florida, officers are doing sweeps for suffering animals in the heat.

"Take this dog for example, a female pitbull named Diamond. Animal care and control has her now. She was seized last week, after authorities took photos of her tied up outside in the heat in a yard in West Palm Beach. The temperature that day was a sweltering 93 degrees and Diamond had no shade, except for a small dog house.

Captain Walesky said, "we try and explain to 'em it's a bad idea, but not only is it a bad idea, it's a law. You can't do this. In Palm Beach County, it's illegal to tie a dog up outside between 10 in the morning and 5 in the evening."

Having a law enables the officers to do what is right and just and what people are asking them to do: save the dog's life, and stop the suffering.

But while most Pennsylvania residents 'get it,' there's still that 10-20% who just don't get it, and need to have their actions legislated. I don't care if you're intelligent or not, you have two eyes, and it's time you open them and your heart and have a good look around at the suffering of chained dogs and the suffering of neighbors forced to endure watching it.

This message on the DDB Facebook fanpage shows the typical ignorance we fight: *"I'd like to know what your alternative is for an outside dog other than chaining? We had a beagle and he was an outside dog for 16 years chained to a doghouse with shade, food, water, and attention several times of day. He broke his chain several times and ran to neighbors luckily or would have been run over by traffic...or a train. In late years, was blind and deaf. Isn't it just as cruel to pen up a large dog in a 3X5 cage in a house for 12-16 hours a day, lying in their feces and urine? What about their rights? What about the handicapped persons in nursing homes who have to sit in a wheelchair or bed for most of their day? Are you standing up for them too?"*

This message is so problematic on many levels. First, it attempts to confuse, by dragging in totally unrelated issues and assuming that it's our responsibility to advocate for all societal wrongs: "What about the handicapped persons in nursing homes who have to sit in a wheelchair or bed for most of their day?"

Second, it states their beagle was an 'outside' dog. If you look in any of the breed books, there is no such thing as an 'outside dog;' these are just regular dogs of every different breed, every single one of which has many others just like it living inside as part of a family. The only difference is the level of responsibility assumed for that dog's happiness and well-being by the dog's caretakers.

Third, she states that: "for 16 years chained to a doghouse with shade, food, water, and attention several times of day." Attention several times a day? My arse! I'm 100% sure that dog was lucky to get any food/water on a daily basis, let alone attention several times a day. Every chainer tries to make out like THEIR dog is the exception to the rule that chained dogs are neglected, and puts a beauty of a spin on it so it appears like the dog led a dandy of a life. In truth, any dog spending 24 hours a day on a chain is by that very virtue neglected and in my opinion abused.

Fourth, she says "He broke his chain several times and ran to neighbors luckily or would have been run over by traffic...or a train." My question is, if he were so happy there, why was he breaking his chain? Why was he running to the neighbors? Maybe because he was seen there and treated with love and respect?

Fifth, she tells us, "In late years, he was blind and deaf." There is no mention that in those years he was indeed given a reprieve from the chain due to his immense physical challenges, but it appears that he was left chained, unable to see, and unable to hear. I can imagine very few greater horrors than to not only be unable to see and hear, but to be nothing more than a sitting duck for any animal or human intending to do you harm. You may smell him coming, but without seeing or hearing, there is no way you could avoid him or fight him off. You are totally vulnerable to death at each and every moment, and without love or light to guide you and give you safety, death would indeed come as a welcome release from the crushing fear.

Sixth, she implies that there is only one alternative to chaining your dog outside: "Isn't it just as cruel to pen up a large dog in a 3X5 cage in a house for 12-16 hours a day, lying in their feces and urine?" Why in God's name would any human with an ounce of decency cage a dog for 12-16 hours in his own feces and urine? Who wouldn't take their dog out to the bathroom? Did you not know that crates are to be used only as tools and only as long as it takes to get the dog trained, then the dog can have the run of the house without incident? What about your dog living in your home with you as a companion, not a prisoner? What about building a fence so your dog can go outside to potty and then come back inside with his pack? Have you heard of walking a dog on a leash? Why are none of these humane possibilities even thought of as an option?

And lastly, she states: "What about their rights?" Here's the one place we agree, Anita, because that's exactly what I want to know. WHAT ABOUT THEIR RIGHTS?

Having just spent five 10-hour days on a chain on their behalf, I'm asking that same question of my state legislators. WHAT

ABOUT THEIR RIGHTS? Despite having endured one week of absolute and mind-numbing 10-hour days of torture on that chain, I still cannot fully comprehend the horror of being there ad infinitum. I so looked forward every day to the magic hour of six o'clock, and I watched as the minutes and seconds dragged on. What if getting off the chain were not an option? What would I do?

I can honestly say I've never waited for a weekend more in my entire 46 years—EVER—and I've pledged to enjoy every single second of my freedom before I force myself back on that chain on Monday. To think that these dogs cannot look forward to freedom for any amount of time is truly unconscionable. I cannot endure the mere thought of it for their sakes.

Pennsylvania legislators, I am holding you accountable for opening your eyes and seeing the suffering of our friends. I am asking those 80-90% of PA citizens who agree with me to join me in holding them accountable.

It's time for this abuse to end, and it's time for people like Anita to grow up, and go buy a dog book for Pete's sake. Some things are common sense, and if you don't have any, then don't have a dog or find a way to buy some. Common sense, that is.

Pennsylvania, and the world, MUST stop tolerating this abuse of Man's Best Friend. If this is how we treat our best friend, I would hate to see how we treat our enemies.

Random incidents or thoughts from the day:

1. My new friend Cathie MacArthur brought me water, sun chips, and magazines. I told her I wasn't allowing myself to read as it wouldn't be fair to the dogs, but I would save the chips for later. She's a very sweet and caring woman.

2. A young girl who works at the Capitol brought me out a bag of pretzels and a water. I wonder if she read my blog from yesterday? Oops!

3. Oddly, by sheer coincidence, an Altoona man I met at a Sheetz one time came wondering by. When I met him before, he was very interested in getting involved, so I had him go to a street in Blandburg, Cambria County (Senator Wozniak's district) where there was a chained dog at every house, and see if he could do any ejumakatin'. He told me that he was physically threatened there by the residents when he tried to discuss their dogs with them. He described it as 'a scary place, man.' Ah, welcome to my world!

4. Deb Smith came and chained up with me for a couple of hours. She was very excited because her house rep hasn't been supportive of chaining legislation, but she is being challenged in the upcoming election by Gene Stilp. She spoke to Gene, and he's fully in support of the legislation, so she called Sue Helms and told her that. Her office immediately said she'd call Deb back on Monday. We all need to push the issue with our reps. Enough is enough.

5. A college student at Harrisburg Area Community College was inspired to do her speech on the issue after seeing the news articles this week. She came to interview me, and was super excited about making a difference and spreading the word that chaining has to stop.

6. Joe surprised me in his beautiful Camaro around 3:00, took me to dinner at 6:00, and played professional photographer, again. How did I ever live without this man?

7. So many of you in the Harrisburg area are bringing me water, worrying about me all day (just like the dogs), and wanting in some way to make a difference. I truly am in awe of your kind-

ness, and humbled by it. Thank you.

8. Color me red-ly embarrassed! What I thought was blood in my urine and a bladder infection was actually red from the beet juice in the veggie drink I got at the corner Juicy Rumors each day! My test from Tuesday night came back fine, and I got suspicious it could be the beet juice, when it happened again, and I was right. Well, at least now we all know...if you drink beet juice, and it turns red, don't panic like I did.

From an online blog: "It's quite normal for the wee to turn red on consuming large amounts of beetroot juice. It's rare to find someone whose wee doesn't turn red after consuming beetroot juice. Mine does, and I've been raw for two years (100%)."

Deb Smith and I, both chained in solidarity

Enjoy your weekend, everyone. Please, if you haven't contacted your Senator yet, it's SO important. Make the call on Monday. Thank you!

Day 6
When a Cicada is the Most Interesting Part of Your Day

August 9

☟☜

Drawing the number 6 on my doghouse, how many to go?

I wonder if we should have a contest for most boring job. I'm pretty sure I'd win. Chained to a doghouse 10 hours a day? Come on…it's a no-brainer.

I was pretty sure early on that the most interesting part of today would be the cicada watching, and turned out I was right.

That's when you know it's bad; real bad.

I was sitting on the steps trying to soak up the last few minutes of Joe's shade before he left, when our 14-year-old friend Morgan, from the Juicy Rumors store on the corner, told us to look out behind us.

Along came a bee, a big bee, heading straight for us and buzzing along the ground dragging a cicada that was even bigger than him. First of all, I didn't know there were any cicadas out this year, and second of all, we hightailed it off the steps and let this thing go about his business before he tried to drag us along too.

Turns out that was probably a very smart move, given that he had a penchant for climbing up anything that got in his way. I could shudder at the thought of him crawling up my back, his little buzzers going and the skritch skritch of the dead cicada rubbing along the material of my shirt. Yuk.

Since it was only 9:30 a.m., I was chained to a doghouse in the immediate vicinity, and none of us had anything better to do, we all took to watching him to see how he would accomplish the particularly daunting mission he had taken upon himself.

He zoomed past us along the ground, and then started crawling up my "Support HB1435" sign. When he made it to the top—about three feet high—he launched himself off, obviously of the mind that he just needed some distance and lift to carry his larger-than-life cargo through the air and get it to his unknown destination faster.

Didn't work out for him.

He made it only three feet before hitting the ground again, cicada still clutched in his determined little bee claws. Undeterred, he continued another five feet, whereupon he came across the green lamppost, and—you guessed it—began to ascend up the pole. We thought maybe he had a nest up there he was taking his prize to, but about halfway up he lost the cicada, which, being dead, tumbled to the sidewalk. He buzzed about frantically, convinced he just needed to find it and all would be well again.

Morgan—being the kindly girl she is—threw the cicada into his path, at which point he latched onto for dear life and decided to take a new tack.

He jumped off the curb and unaware of the immediate danger to his personage, started across traffic to the other side of the street. He somehow, like in Frogger, managed to survive the grinding wheels of about five autos before reaching the other side, climbing up the mailbox, and launching himself into the air again.

Still didn't work out for him.

Now he dragged his cicada to the edge of the building wall, narrowly missed being crunched by numerous pairs of human shoes, and started up the side of the State Street Building. He did pretty well until he hit about 12 feet up, where the building jutted outward instead of inward.

This obstacle proved to be his undoing. He tried and tried to drag the cicada around the decorative edging but science and gravity were against him. He just couldn't do it. Frustrated (at least so my super-sensitive bee-psychic powers told me), he flew back down into the street he'd just come from, dropped his cicada, and aborted his mission.

Joe claimed he was going back to headquarters to tell them he didn't find anything.

I'd like to claim there to be some big, uplifting moral to this story. Like "If at first you don't succeed, fail and fail some more, until you fail so badly your bug gets smushed on the road and you finally beat a hasty retreat," but somehow that just doesn't sound very convincing, or uplifting.

I guess you'll have to make one up for yourself.

The one thing I know for sure about this story is that what drove me to watch it unfold is still happening day after day in backyards all across America, and most definitely here in Pennsylvania.

Dogs are so damn bored, hot, and miserable on the chain that they are chasing bugs and are limited to being spectators in their own lives, never getting the chance to actually live one for themselves.

You and I have the chance now to make a difference for these dogs. Work on this law with me, call your Senator, and insist that he/she support SB1435. Chained dogs deserve better than to put 'bug-watcher' on their resume. They deserve instead to put 'family member,' 'ball-fetcher,' and 'car-rider-with-tongue-hanging-and-ears-flapping.'

Oh, yeah!

Miscellaneous postings from the day:

1. My mom always told me there'd be days like this. I don't think she did, but seemed like a good place to insert that phrase. I'm pretty sure she never told me there'd be days I was chained

to a doghouse at the PA state Capitol, being bored to death and roasting my butt off. My poor mother!

2. I repeated DDB Rep Melody's Whitworth's experiment with the thermometer in the doghouse. This being wooden, it didn't get quite as hot as the plastic one she used, but it was still consistently five degrees higher than the outside temp. We reached a high of 97 degrees today, and the doghouse 102 degrees. I wonder who really thinks that a doghouse provides a dog with shade or some kind of cooling? You can download the flyer to post around from the volunteer page on our website.

3. Thank Dog the concrete on the steps and sidewalk are a very light gray. Where the trim around the edges is a bit darker, there is a VERY noticeable difference in temperature.

4. The sky was virtually cloud-free all day. Not really good for me.

5. My pants were black and lined, which will be great on a cooler day, but today, they were absolutely unbearable. I was hoping I didn't lose it, rip them off, and go running down the street in my skivvies. Skivvies. I like that word.

6. There was just a small area of shade behind the sign and pylon, measuring about 1' by 2.' I decided to go stand there to see if it was cooler. It was probably a good 10 to 20 degrees cooler! I told myself I would stand in the spot, but I wouldn't sit down in it, that was too undignified. But soon my feet hurt so bad from standing that I ended up scrunched at the bottom of the pylon into a little ball, trying to stay within the boundaries of the shade. I didn't even care what I looked like to passersby. It was a matter of survival at that point. I stayed there scrunched up until the shade from the building across the street hit me around 3:30.

7. Tomorrow's supposed to be hotter and more humid. I'm hoping I can endure it.

Gordon Bakalar, the man HATES chaining!

8. Thanks to my friends who've been so supportive, and my supporters turned friends who are bringing me water, Gatorade, ice, give bathroom breaks. You rock.

Huddled in a small patch of shade. Screw dignity! This is life or death.

Day 7
I Wrote You a Poem

August 10

☙❧

Alison Pollock is chained, and wanted to help take a stand for the dogs

Today was just SO stupendously boring that I wrote you a poem. You don't have to thank me. Your adoration of my extreme poetic skill is all the thanks I need.

The Chained Tami Poem

This is a blog
About a dog
House, that is.

To which I am chained
But never complain
Much, that is.

For truth be told
Be I so bold,
Sucks, it does.

It's raging hot
I sweat a lot
Bullets, they are.

But here I'll sit
Taking shit
For them, I will.

They Deserve Better
So write a letter
Begging, I am.

It's not for me
For them I plea
Suffering, they are.

"We're here for their law"
Just give us your paw
Free them, we will.

Live in PA? Have you told your Senator to vote YES on anti-tethering yet? Please give the dogs five minutes of your time to save them a lifetime of suffering.

Day 7, Temp outside, 96 Degrees, Temp in Doghouse, 102 Degrees

Miscellaneous and oh so boring stuff from today:

1. OK, it's so freakin' hot! Have I said that before? I don't think it can be said enough. I'm going to have to say it once for every chained dog in PA since they don't have a voice.

2. It was already 90 degrees at 11:00 a.m. Every last ounce of shade was gone at that time, not to come back until 3:30 p.m.

3. Will miracles never cease! A crotchety older guy who has walked by me a hundred times and ignored me each time talked to me! He told me he'd get me a book that has all the senators and reps pics in it so I could recognize them. Granted, he might not get it for me if he reads this and knows I referred to him as

crotchety, but he probably isn't reading my blog; or, if so, he will be so floored by my poem that he can't even go on reading. It's understandable.

[Oops! He must have read my blog, he totally went back to ignoring me and never did give me the book.]

Self-Portrait in Sweat

4. There was a point today where I really just didn't think I could go on. I wondered if it was even doing any good. But I believe in cosmic good vs. paper good…and somewhere, on a cosmic level, the gods know that I'm making a huge sacrifice for the chained dogs, and they will send a lightning bolt to create a miracle. Either that or Zac Efron with his sword-pen will slay us some dragons. I'm pretty convinced. Don't rain on my parade.

$\mathcal{D}ay\ 8$
I am Controlled by the Weather, Bah!

August 11

Stacey brought me flowers, so we proclaimed me Miss Chained Dog America.
Yes, I was the only contestant, but who's counting.

I searched frantically within the chain's reach for some shade, knowing I would find none.

Day 8 marked the third day with temps of 95 and above, not a cloud in the sky, and the heat index reaching 98 or more. There were times throughout the past three days when I just didn't know if I could go on, could last that elusive four hours between morning and afternoon shade.

My shade schedule is as follows:

8:00 a.m. I first hit the Capitol and my spot at the bottom of the steps. The sun is just peeking over the top of the building. I have shade for about 15 minutes as it continues to slowly wake up the Capitol.

8:00 a.m.-10:00 a.m. I suck it up, sitting in my spot or talking to passersby, or pacing and dragging my chain. The heat continues to climb, but it's not yet unbearable.

10:00 a.m. On Day 6 I discovered that the 3-foot high wall facing the street has shade from my waist down until about 11:15. I drag my chain over and stand against the wall. I can't sit or do much else there due to it being the sidewalk, so it's a bit awkward. Yesterday a guy stopped and offered me a ride. I politely declined, seeing as how my chain wouldn't have gotten us very far without dragging a doghouse down the road along with us.

11:15 a.m.-3:30 p.m. After 11:15, I'm pretty well screwed until 3:30, unless I've snookered someone into getting the big sign Darryl made me out of the van, which is big enough to create the speck of shade around the concrete pylon. If so, there may be as little as a 1' by 2' patch of shade for me to huddle in, and I do, all thoughts of dignity gone from my head. I'm that desperate.

I suffer very much during this time, and I know the dogs do too. You just can't help it. Your whole world revolves around the fact that the heat is unbearable and how you are supposed to make it through. I don't read or listen to music to distract me, because I want the experience to be as authentic as I can make it. But I am truly miserable, and you would never convince me a dog left out in that heat isn't as well.

I watch as the shade encroaches on the sun's territory. Starting at 2:30 the sun begins to be blocked by the tall State Street building across the street. Thank Dog for that tall building! I wait impatiently for it to hit my sitting area.

After the shade hits, I feel I've successfully made it through the day. The absolutely tortuous part is over, and the rest seems like a walk in the park by comparison. Unfortunately, it's another 1/2 hour before I can comfortably sit without my butt cheeks feeling like they are burning off. The cement is that hot.

I am suddenly obsessed with the weather forecast, checking Weatherbug a week in advance (like they're EVER accurate that far ahead) because I feel a huge need to be warned about what I have to endure. I need to mentally prepare myself.

I know that chained dogs probably don't do the worrying that I'm capable of, but you can't tell me they don't know every patch of shade that they may or may not find in the unbearable summer heat. And if they find none? They probably resort to pacing the way I do to stop myself from going crazy in the heat of mid-day.

I wanted to make sure you know that dogs cannot sweat like people do, and so are less able to withstand the heat than I am, or you are. They must pant to get their bodies to let off steam.

But if they have no shade, no water, and it's 97 degrees? They often expire and are usually dumped without officials or animal advocates being able to prove any neglect on the part of the caretaker.

SB1435 would prohibit chaining without access to at least one shady spot (besides their doghouse) and not in temps of 90 or above. (Based on my experience this should go down 10 degrees.)

We are these dogs only hope of getting these concessions which could very well save their lives. They need us. They need a voice, and we are all they have.

Let's put a stop to this ridiculous cruelty by passing SB1435, a step in the right direction.

Thoughts for the day:

1. It was a weird day at the Capitol. First two guys started whaling on each other down by the guard shack, who knows why. The Capitol policeman came out and got them broken up. Then a car was driving on the opposite side of the street, and almost had a head-on with someone driving the right way. Luckily the blaring of the horn caused him to swerve over and then get back into his correct lane.

2. A big thank you to CPAA who helped get me a greatly discounted room at the Radisson starting next week! Everyone, if you're ever traveling to Harrisburg for business, please choose the Radisson…if they support the important work of your fellow dog advocate, we need to make sure we support them too.

3. I felt really bad today when Gordon and Mike were hanging out with me in the super hot weather. I didn't like to see them suffering, and I know that many of you don't like to see me suffering either.

Let's use this suffering to get everyone motivated to call their Senators! I only need five minutes of your time, make the call. Find your senator here: http://www.legis.state.pa.us/

Day 9
I Bit a Child Today

August 12

A horrendous storm toward the end of the day did both me and the city in.

bit a child today.

I spend my life at the end of a chain, so to me this thing called "child" is nothing more than prey or an underling I neither love nor respect. Maybe it squeaks like an animal, or makes quick movements that I don't understand or frightens me and triggers my flight or fight instinct.

I cannot flee. I'm chained. Fleeing is therefore not an option for me, so I must fight.

You never taught me how to live in your world, yet you expect me to abide by its rules.

I bit a child today.

You got me as a puppy and I chewed something up. You tossed me aside with your doghouse and chain.

I'm a big dog. What breed am I? Doesn't matter. Wait, I know my breed: the chained dog. We come in all shapes and sizes, but I'll tell you one thing we're not: a beloved family pet.

I bit a child today.

I am unsocialized with humans. I don't recognize a small child as human, not a valued member of your clan. I sit on this logging chain day in and day out, come sun, rain, sleet, or snow. I am male, unneutered, and chained, and am three times more likely to be aggressive than any other dog.

I am full of pent-up energy from never getting to run or stretch my legs, pent-up sexual frustration from a constant and unfulfilled urge to mate, and pent-up anger from living a solitary life when I'm meant to live as part of your pack.

I have been domesticated by man to be a partner to man, a companion to man, a helper to man. Yet man is so disconnected from himself that he sees nothing wrong with chaining me to this doghouse and abandoning me here to die.

I bit a child today.

This is my territory. I have no life except to guard my solitary patch of dirt. If you cross into my territory despite my warnings, there is a good chance I will attack you to protect myself and the dirt I see as mine.

I bit a child today.

Now they've come with a big pole, they're taking me away; I'm scared, and I don't know what I did wrong.

I bit a child today, and now I will die.

You have made me thus, and now both the child and I have paid your price.

Chained dogs DO attack and kill children. On Monday, August 9, a toddler was attacked by a chained dog that broke free in Philadelphia, Pennsylvania. We need laws limiting chaining to better socialize our dogs and better protect our children from aggressive dogs.

Miscellaneous events of the day:

1. I couldn't even tweet about the pouring rain because, well, I was in the pouring rain! It was crazy, I tell you, crazy.

2. Special thanks to Daly Gonzalez, a Temple student who came out to film today. Not only did she do a great job filming

for her project, but got herself pretty darn wet staying out in the rain to film and photograph me. I hope your project gets an A, Daly! You deserve it.

3. The workers at Sammy's Restaurant across the street ignored me until the rain came today...then they came out to gawk, laugh, and take pictures. Nice!

4. Apparently some of the city streets flooded, and the traffic was a nightmare...it took 40 minutes to get back to the hotel instead of 10. Sirens were going off like crazy...And there I stood, chained to a doghouse in the midst of it all. Of course I could have walked away—but the dogs can't, so I didn't either.

Day 10
Finally, Entertainment!

August 13

😊😊

The two factions start to line up, and I was standing chained in the middle

I've created a video of the 'highlights' of the first ten days of my chaining and a plea to support anti-chaining legislation for all PA residents. You can view it at: http://www.youtube.com/watch?v=LaGPgCclc6M. No matter what state you're in or what year it is as you read this book, if you don't have anti-tethering legislation, fight for it. These dogs deserve it.

Some thoughts from this week:

1. Wow. The weather couldn't have been much worse. First, three days of 95 plus temps, then a deluge the next day that flooded the city, and I was standing out in it the whole time. Then, even today it rained a slow steady soaking rain for the first two hours, and drizzled off and on throughout the rest of the day.

2. Today, I got MAJORLY excited when the people who are against same-sex marriages held a rally and the supporters of same-sex marriages lined up across the street. I was just like the chained dog at the family picnic…along the edges, not being noticed, but still excited to have ANYTHING different to do other than the total boredom of my day!

The rally and counter-protest took up two hours, and there was a ton of people-watching to be had. I smiled the whole time. Silly, really, but when you're the chained dog, you quickly learn how important any kind of stimulation is to your sensibility.

The funniest part was that people thought I was part of the rally, and they were so confused as to what message I was putting out by being chained to a doghouse! I paced, dragging my chain the whole time they were speaking just because I could.

4. I chose pizza and fried mushrooms for my 6:00 meal, and boy was it yummy. This time I got smarter and took some enzymes to digest my food; so far, no belly ache.

5. I'm home with my dogs for the first time in two weeks, they really missed mommy! I told them I'm doing it for their people, but not sure if they understand.

Day 11
I'm All About the 11

August 16

Trying to find shade between 11:00 a.m. and 3:00 p.m.

The number 11 has been my favorite number for years. My daughter Brynnan always asks me what my favorite number is, and I always say the same thing. If you've studied numerology at all, and noticed the fascinating "coincidences" that come into play around numbers, you can't help but become intrigued by the power you can find therein.

Eleven is the number of vision, inspiration, and illumination.

Since 11 is my number, today I sat for the dogs in Blair County, which is the county I live in. *I still see dogs chained there every day despite our best efforts, and there's not a damn thing I can do about it.*

I cannot measure the amount of frustration that fact causes me.

But, despite how mind-numbingly boring and frustrating is the act of sitting here chained day in and day out, **it is also incredibly empowering and powerful.**

For six years we've been working to bring some kind of relief to dogs on chains. Yet all the power has been in the hands of the legislators, people who know nothing of the issue and too often don't care about the suffering these dogs are enduring. When they have chosen to ignore requests to support the bill from constituents, DDB, and other supporters, I, along with everyone I know, felt incredibly powerless.

I felt like I had no voice, you had no voice, and these dogs certainly had no voice. We were not heard.

But since I came here I have stopped my own personal cycle of powerlessness. By taking action, by making it clear in no uncertain terms what I want to happen and sacrificing my own daily life to go for it, I have taken back my personal power.

I still can't control what they do. But I can control what I do, and I'm chained here to say NO MORE!

After today, I will have spent eleven 10-hour days on a chain. That adds up to 110 hours. Impressive, I think to myself....So I decide to calculate how many hours a dog spends chained if he lives for 11 years. **That would be 11 times 365 days times 24 hours, for a grand total of 96,360 hours.**

On a CHAIN! No dog deserves that!

Suddenly, my own feat dwindles and my resolve stiffens.

96,360 hours. What a travesty. We've GOT to get this done.

Miscellaneous thoughts from the day:

1. My Gatorade bottle had something on it that the ants liked. I was so bored that I began studying the ant culture, and I noticed that the big ant, while he looks much stronger and intimidating, is actually afraid of the little ants, and they keep driving him away. Remember this pertains to us as well. The senators may seem big and scary, but they need us to vote for them in order to stay in office. We have a lot more power than we know, especially en masse. We deserve this law, and so do the dogs.

2. Even Steve, the Juicy Rumors owner, took most of the day off. I get it. It's Monday, who wants to work (or be chained) on a Monday?

3. My ankle is really swollen. I haven't gone to the doctor about it, but first twisted it when Joe and I were walking down the mountain where we hike with the dogs. I told him it was no big deal, I have sturdy ankles (he keeps saying stout...no, honey, I never said stout) and they bounce right back. Me and my big mouth. It seemed to be healing, but then I aggravated it out here on Friday somehow, and Joe bought me an ankle brace on Saturday. I was afraid I'd be having to use crutches; it hurt that bad. But Sunday it was feeling better, so I went without the brace today, and now I'm regretting that move.

Day 12
Unbridled Frustration

August 17

A sprain aggravation forces me to wear an ankle brace. Tres chic!

Day 12 promised to be an easy day weather-wise, a relief from the rain of Days 9-11, yet I still felt that I'd hit a wall. If I had to stay chained for even one more second I thought I would implode and explode all at the same time!

The pent-up energy and need to do SOMETHING, anything but sit here bored shitless for ten hours was pecking away at my insides, and my new hat and ankle brace were doing little to keep

91

it under wraps.

The intense sun of Days 6-8 baked my skin despite the 100 SPF sunblock I'd been using, and I had grown fearful that the part in my hair where I couldn't put sunscreen would become so burned I would expose myself to skin cancer.

It reminded me of one of New Mexico Area Rep Amanda Barnett's chained rescues, a white pittie, that could never be exposed to large amounts of sun again because of all the damage done to his fair skin while chained and ignored in the brutal New Mexico sun by his caretakers.

I realized I would have to break down and buy a hat in order to protect my skin. Today was the debut of said hat, which I'm calling the "Urban Safari," and is serving to make my head even hotter, but at least more protected from the sun's rays.

At the opposite end of the body spectrum I'm holding my ankle together with duct tape (kidding) and a black ankle brace Joe bought for me this weekend when I was whining about the pain in my ankle. It swelled majorly yesterday due to me some-how tweaking it here on Friday afternoon, and I'm hoping to avoid the whole "chained with crutches" look that I'm sure we'd all find super-attractive.

The pent-up energy I'm feeling after only twelves days on the chain speaks volumes of the frustration felt by chained dogs and serves as a big clue as to the mystery of why chained dogs are more aggressive.

Dogs are energetic beings! They are much more energetic than most people and definitely more than I am. Imagine the torture for them when they just want to run, run, run, and instead are confined to a solitary patch of dirt.

I've never felt so in-tune with the emotional and psychological process of the chained dog.

We have to get serious about getting help for these dogs. Lawmakers are here to express the voice of the people. We have to make them hear our voices so that it results in some relief for America's suffering dogs.

Do I keep saying that? Can't help it!

Day 13
Who Do we Want to be, Pennsylvania, America?

August 18

*The chain makes for it's share of jokes, here Stacey Romberger
is trying to get hubby Mike in line...never an easy task, as we women know!*

Today I had my first Russian tourist. This guy was filming away at the Capitol, then turned the camera on me, saying one word "Russian."

"OK," I said, and took him on the doghouse tour, attempting to explain what I was doing here and why. He was with a party of five, and one lady was acting as translator. He finally said "You think dogs here in America have it bad?"

Another girl with them who spoke English told me that in Russia most of the dogs are strays and are beaten by the Russian people when they drink too much.

Their general attitude was "why are you bothering to advocate for dogs here in America, because there are places where they have it worse."

I'll tell you why. Because abuse is abuse, and whether it is seen in 1/4 of the American people or 3/4 of the Russian people, these dogs matter, and the feelings of the people who have to watch the abuse matter.

By contrast, virtually daily (for some unknown reason) around 5:30 in the afternoon an organized tour of 40-50 French citizens comes pouring out of the Capitol. They typically surround my doghouse and me, whispering and staring, trying to figure what the heck I'm up to and why.

I try to find one of them who speaks English, and explain to him/her how dogs are legally allowed to be treated here in America. That it's perfectly acceptable by law for them to be chained for every second of their entire lives on a 50-lb., 6-ft. logging chain, never going for a walk, EVER, never knowing the kindly pat of a hand or having a warm bed to call their own.

The French tourists are universally appalled and horrified that we have continued a practice they've ended many years ago and insist they would never chain their dogs. They tell me it's a good thing I'm taking on, and to keep up the fight for our best friends.

This vast difference between these two societies brings to mind the oft-used quote from Gandhi: "The greatness of a nation and its moral progress can be judged by the way its animals are treated."

I would ask America and Pennsylvania this question: which society do you wanna be? Do you want to take out your anger on a helpless dog who has done you no wrong, treating him/her like a piece of property that can be abused at will, or do you want to treat our companion animals with the respect and dignity they deserve?

Who do you want to be?

A few observations of the day:

1. It was actually a very busy day by chained dog standards. Seemed that every moment was taken up with talking to passersby or friends I've made along the way.

2. The WGAL reporter, Matt Belanger, a real card, told me he wants to get with me for an update. I told him he should do it when it's raining, that's some good footage. Would be good for him; me, not so much…of course the challenge is not getting the camera wet.

3. I'm eternally grateful to my onsite support team: Mike and Stacey Romberger, Gordon Bakalar, Cathie MacArthur, Melissa Swauger, Darryl, Amy, and all those who come by to spend a little time with me or help me load up in the evening. I so appreciate all the bathroom breaks, water, and Gatorade trips you've logged.

Day 14
A Vision for Chained Dogs

August 19

⊙⊙

Just one of my perches, sitting with my back to the sun.

I often do an abundance meditation I learned from Louise Hay's book "You Can Heal Your Life" where I go to the ocean with whatever tool I feel worthy of filling, to partake of the abundance of the universe. The point of the exercise is to help the readers realize that there is plenty for all, that abundance is not just for the chosen few.

Usually I can easily-enough muster up an average-sized bucket, and if I do it regularly, I always see improvement in my finances and in my world.

Today I started the usual meditation as I was sitting alone on my chain and feeling like I needed to open my heart to some good for both myself and DDB.

But to my surprise the meditation changed. I found myself approaching the ocean with a HUGE blue bucket, bigger than me, which I easily filled, put on top of my head, and carried back to the chained dogs. The water turned to a clear, fresh, thirst-quenching blue, and I stopped before each dog and gave him/her a drink from the bucket. I was smiling and full of love for them, and wordlessly passing along the message that they were recognized, valued, and loved, and we would not stop fighting for their rights in our world.

Wow, what a powerful vision! I am truly in awe of and inspired by it, I hope it can inspire you too. How can you tend to the chained dogs near you?

Miscellaneous and sundry thoughts from the day:

1. The people who work at Sammy's Authentic Italian Cuisine have never acknowledged my presence except to take pictures of me with their cell phones in the flooding rain. I'm sure that was with the kindest of intentions, though, and not to make fun of me, right? Therefore I don't feel obligated to plug their restaurant, but I will give them this much: those guys thoroughly clean their windows daily, as well as their outside tables and chairs. From that I would imagine that their restaurant is quite tidy.

2. A candidate for the House from Lancaster County named F. Patrick O'Keeffe stopped by to see me, and pledged to co-sponsor legislation for chained dogs if and when he gets into office. We all know what Lancaster County is famous for...an animal

friendly rep from that county can only be a good thing. Well, an animal friendly rep from any county can only be a good thing.

3. Today was my day for weird encounters with people who are down on their luck. I can't even get into the story Gravy told me, but it was a story of homelessness and violence that shook me to the roots.

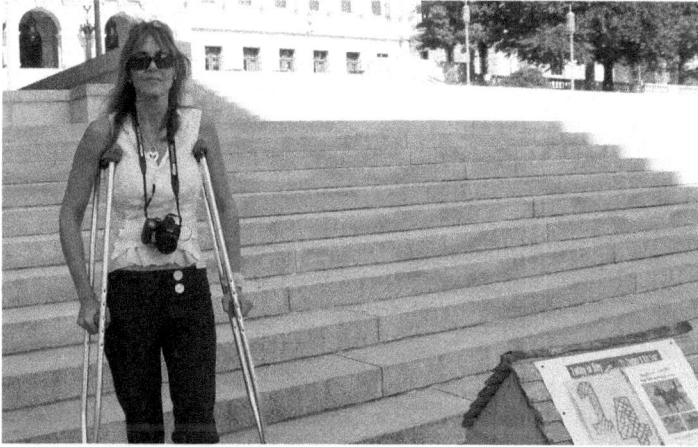

A Chinese man came by, speaking very poor English, and was telling Tina Evangelista-Eppenstein and me about trying to sleep in his car in Gettysburg and being abused by the police. He had just tried to get into see Rendell, but they wouldn't let him in. Turned out he thought I was a reporter and I could get his story in print. I was like, "No, I'm just an activist hanging out here on this chain."

4. Nearly every day about 4:30, a tallish, blonde woman pulls up right in front of me in an SUV, gets out of the drivers seat and moves around to the passenger seat. Despite being only 10 feet away from me, she never speaks to me or looks in my direction. The first day I witnessed her husband come out of work, put his stuff in the back of the vehicle, and get in the driver's seat without either of them speaking a word to each other or looking at each other. I thought it was really odd, but almost every day since the same thing has happened.

Day 15
Would Jesus Chain His Dogs?

August 20

The sun peeks over the Capitol, signifying the start of another day.

I've been on a chain too long. It's already led to aggression.

I thoroughly admit to wanting to bite an older woman today. They had walked by earlier in the morning, three senior-aged ladies, and then walked back in the opposite direction four hours later.

As they walked toward me, they were "Amen"-ing and "Praise the Lord"-ing the man preaching on the corner across the street. That man can project his voice, let me tell ya'!

These women were obviously church-going folk.

They neared me, and the stout, grey-haired lady said to me, "Weren't you here earlier when we walked by?"

I said "Yes, I've been here for fifteen days, I'm chained to win a law for the dogs."

She said, "Oh, that's ridiculous, some dogs like it out there."

I admit it. My blood boiled, and yes, I wanted to bite her.

I explained ever so gently to her that that was a load of crap, that dogs are pack animals, and that they want to be with humans. They don't want to live on chains.

She continued to go at me, and I finally told her to go across the street and actually listen the preacher over there that she was so busy Amen-ing before. Hopefully he would be preaching something about kindness to all living beings.

She flounced off in a huff, and the two ladies with her told me they agreed that dogs shouldn't live on chains. They said their dogs lived inside, and that their neighbors had dogs outside which they pitied.

I'm hoping they stood their ground when she continued her onslaught in the car, but she was quite a forceful old biddy. She probably has them rushing off home to chain their dogs up as we speak.

Unfortunately, I see this all too often in the religious community—although many people of God, including my immediate family, would no longer consider such a thing. Religious people who claim to love and care for others as God intends, but defend animal cruelty and show no concern for the suffering of the dogs in their care really do their religions a great disservice.

Who would want to be part of this woman's church? Certainly not me.

I believe that if they asked themselves in their hearts "Would Jesus chain his dogs?" and listened carefully to the answer, they'd be out in their yard unchaining their dogs and treating them immediately with the care and respect they deserve.

Think about it. Would Jesus chain his dog? As one who's read the Bible three times, I say an emphatic "I think not."

Today, I saw these interesting Harrisburgites:

1. My friend the American of Mayan descent, who's on parole but seems to be a very intelligent, gifted man. He's always so friendly, laughing, and joking.

2. My friend the American of Chinese descent, who was apparently trying to get into see Rendell at the Capitol again. More power to him. Don't give up!

3. My friend Steve who rides his Harley without a helmet, saying, "Well, I made it to 50."

4. My friend Tom, who teared up the first day as he described the chained dogs he sees along his route to work.

5. The married couple, who are youngish by the way, only mid-30's I'd guess, who don't speak or look at each other. Today they said a few words, I wonder if they read the blog and knew it was them? Nah.

6. And my new friend Cathie MacArthur, who brought me her world-famous lentil salad for 6:00 p.m. Dang, that was some good stuff!

For the record, just to make things REALLY clear, I'm really, really tired of being so hot and sweaty. I'm 100% sure that each and every time in the future days of my life that I am outside and I get hot and sweaty, I will have flashbacks to these days of chaining at the Capitol. And cringe.

I'm here for YOU, dogs...let's get it done.

Day 16
Let Me Entertain You

August 23

A group of musicians come along and make up some awesome chained dog songs

I asked my boyfriend Joe this morning if he read my Day 15 blog. He said, "No, why, was there something funny in there?"

Now, I love my beau dearly, he's my Edward except without the endless youth and superpowers (sorry, baby—maybe next life), but I'm still thinking, "What, you only read my blog if it's funny now?"

Oh, the pressure to keep my man laughing! How can I possibly make my quest to free chained dogs funnier?

And more entertaining?

Here in America we ARE all about our entertainment, of course. Nothing much else matters.

Someone once wanted to do a TV show with me. Turned out I wasn't edgy enough.

Sitting here on the Capitol steps, I'm pretty sure I'm too edgy for these legislative types.

In fact, just today I saw my senator, Eichelberger, drive by in his blue pickup truck with bumper stickers all over the back and he just stared at me. [You're staring at me? At least I don't have a bumpkin truck.]

I imagine he was thinking *"Why, oh why does she have to be MY constituent?"*

I'm definitely too edgy for THAT man!

But the bottom line is I'm really not here to entertain anyone. What I AM here for is a law for my clients, the dogs I fight for each day.

These dogs are why I sit here every day, bored senseless, and oh so miserable on a million different levels.

And what I need, to be very clear, is to convince YOU how much they need and deserve this law, so we as a group can convince THEM (the legislators) how much they need and deserve this law.

So what will it take to get you to contact the members of the Ag Committee ASAP to ask them to move the bill to the floor for a vote?

I did almost get a picture of a guy today laying on the ground behind his motorcycle (or was it a scooter?) trying to get a pic of it with the Capitol in the background. That probably would have been enough to entertain Joe, since he has three motorcycles, but you? Maybe not so much.

Other entertaining or not so much stuff from today:

1. Woman walking down the street: "Do you think they care? I seen you on TV, and I know you tryin', but they don't give a damn." Me: "Thanks for the encouragement!"

2. A few different Senate workers came by today as a result of a wtif.org news piece that was on the radio this morning. They couldn't believe that dog chaining for life was still legal to begin with!

3. The weather was peachy-keen today. Oops, did I say peaches? Yes, the peach ladies were back, and I admit to finding them more and more annoying. I need to bless them instead; I hope those were the best peaches EVER. (Actually, I think they might have been apples today, as they were talking about making sauce, but they will forever be known to me as the Peach Ladies regardless of what free fruit they are filling up their little bags with today.)

4. A traveling group of teenage band members, going by the name Chapel Ave stopped and played for me. They made up hilarious chained dogs songs on the spur of the moment, I posted them on YouTube. What a hoot.

5. Many people who aren't familiar with chaining as a social issue mistakenly think we want to do away with leashes. THAT would be mayhem! I explain to them that leashes have a person on the other end who is sharing the bond of the walk, and

chains have a pole (or other inanimate object) on the other end where the dog remains for the bulk of his/her life, alone and unsocialized.

6. DDB supporter and friend Melissa Swauger stopped by a local thrift store and fixed me up with some more nice clothes for me to ruin by being chained out here. Totally cool.

Day 17
I've Got MAIL!

August 24

👀

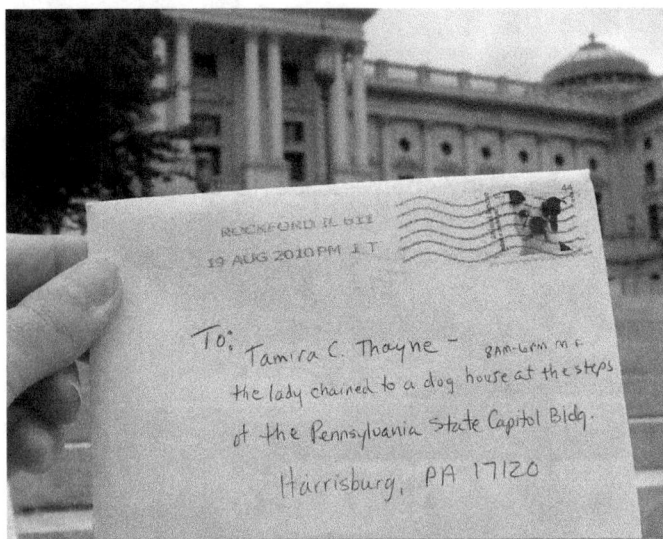

I wish it was delivered by an owl...you know, like in Harry Potter? That would rock.

Today I got a piece of mail delivered to me by the Capitol mailman, addressed to "Tamira Thayne, the lady chained to a doghouse at the steps, Pennsylvania State Capitol Building, Harrisburg, PA 17120."

The mailman and I both ended up giggling after he bemusedly walked up to me and said he assumed this was me, handing me a card from a supporter in Illinois.

I have jokingly talked about getting a mailbox for my 'area,' and have indeed become very territorial about it. The last two mornings I've come into a complete mess in my spot (in fact, it's still quite untidy) and I'm heavily considering purchasing a little broom and dustpan, because it's driving me crazy living in all this filth. I have a conspiracy theory going that the senators are sending out their aids in the morning to junk it up before I get here. Can't get rid of me that easy!

I've seen chained dogs living in mud up to their shins, and amongst junk and so much garbage you have to scour to pick out the dog. I guess this place doesn't compare to that, but it's become quite untidy.

Getting this piece of mail here today really cheered me up and legitimized the 17 days I've undergone chained to this doghouse. It reminded me of our Valentine campaign, where we mail Valentines to chained dogs all over the country, and how I wish they knew we were out here fighting for them so hard and loving them so fiercely.

Barb Nozzi, you made my day! Thanks for taking my mailbox comments seriously enough to send out a card and donation to me here. I hope I can give you a big hug in person for your caring act someday.

Miscellaneous craziness from the day:

1. It was downright chilly today. It's making me realize how few truly perfect days there are, how many more cold days to come, and probably more hot ones too.

2. The preachers were back. Four guys all took turns reading the Bible across the street, three of them could really project their voices. One even walked across the street to give me a flyer, so I had Stacey give him one in return when she walked back to the office.

3. Someone came out from the Capitol and told me she'd been hearing about me and she was grateful that there were people in the world who cared enough to act.

4. The afternoon was crazy busy talking to people, and just flew by, unlike the afternoons of the dogs stuck in the backyards across Pennsylvania. I was the lucky 'dog' today.

5. Mike said that he sent a letter too last Thursday from Harrisburg, but that one didn't show up.

Day 18
We've got to 'Bru' it UP!

August 25

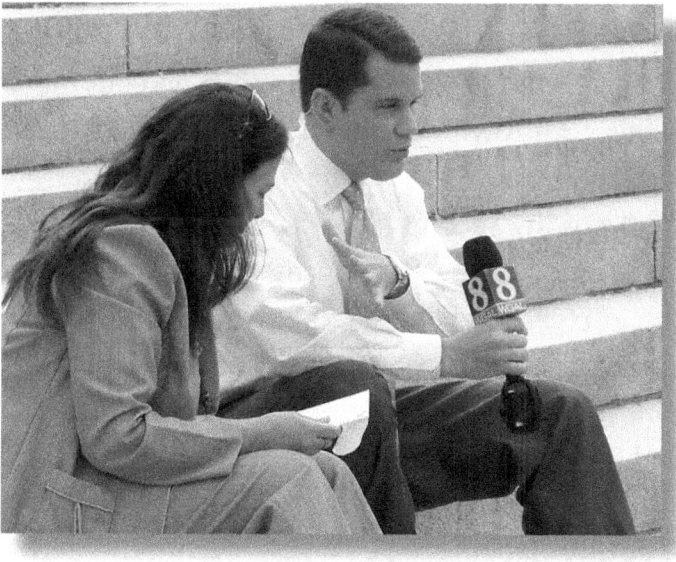

Matt Belanger from Channel 8 does another interview because of the mail

My new Capitol friend (I say that a lot, I know, but I've met a ton of very caring people here!) Darryl made me flyers focusing on AG Committee Chair Mike Brubaker to hand out while I sit here.

Both he and a Capitol "insider" told me that Brubaker's the man we need to concentrate on to move the bill out of committee.

I know this isn't the exciting stuff, but I've learned in my eight years of working for chained dogs that it's about 90% picking up poop (and the such-like) and 10% love, kisses, and accolades. You've gotta be in it for the long haul to make a difference, and do a lot of crap work.

If we want a law providing some relief for Pennsylvania's chained dogs, we ALL, yes, YOU, must do the hard work like contacting senators. I know it can be scary and intimidating, but remember that you usually only talk to an aide, and they all put their pants on one leg at a time like we do At least I hope so.

So now we have to bring on the 'Bru', 'Bru' it up, and send those letters, e-mails, and phone calls Mike Brubaker's way, asking him to pass the bill out of committee, and put the bill on the September 15th town hall meeting agenda to which we will all show up.

Today I got my second letter addressed to "Tamira Thayne, the lady chained at the foot of the Capitol steps" from Sandy Harrison in York, PA, and the Capitol mailman told me they now have a box for me in there. ***A mailbox, in the Capitol! How cool is that?***

WGAL-8's Matt Belanger came out and did a live report on my mail at noon, and as much as I'd love to get more mail from you all on the Capitol steps, I'd love even more knowing Mike Brubaker and the rest of the Senate Ag Committee were being swamped with letters, phone calls, and e-mails.

It all boils down to this. Do you really think dogs deserve to live 24/7 at the end of a chain? I think not. If you agree, PLEASE make your voices heard by this Senate Committee and your local senators.

Show up for this meeting near Lancaster, PA, on September 15, and help me move the bill. I cannot do it alone.

Insanity of the Day

1. Some Amish (or Mennonite) guys walked by on the other side of the Capitol steps. They all stared, and I stared right back. Next thing here they come down the steps, and they stop to ask me what I am doing.

They both have chained dogs, and didn't understand that dogs don't want to live like that. I will give them credit for holding a civil conversation, but I am doubtful that I swayed them that dogs deserve better. The one did ask if he should let his dog off the chain for a bit...I said, yes, that's a step in the right direction.

2. I'm currently considering how to affix a mailbox to my dog-house and still have it be very portable, now that I actually AM getting mail here.

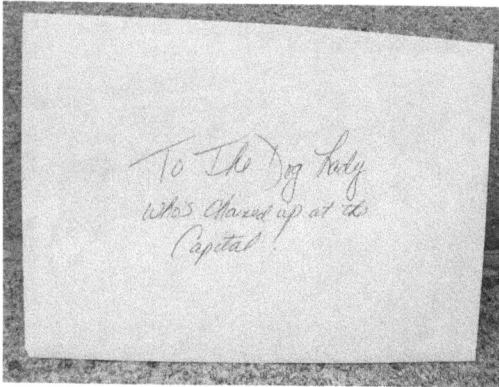

3. Another couple pulled up in a pickup truck and hand-delivered a card. It also was addressed to "the dog lady who's chained up at the Capitol." I might have to change my name again. It's rather lengthy, I know, but if people are starting to know me by that name...

4. I tripped over my chain today, almost fell on my face, and it reminded me of the horrible story featured this week about a dog who got her leg tangled in the chain and chewed it off to get free. What can you even say to a story as awful as that?

Day 19
I Just Want to Play (and so do They)

August 26

☙❦

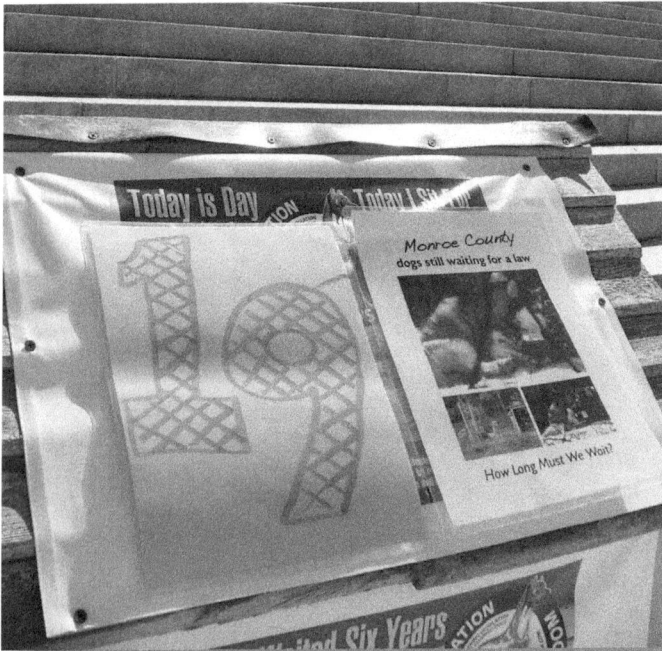

19 Days! Whod'a thunk it.

I know how much you liked the last poem, so I wrote you another one, which is even worse. My 11-year-old daughter can probably write better poetry! Enjoy it, you're welcome.

My boyfriend's coming today.
I really want to go play.
But alas, I'm here to stay.
8-6, every weekday.

At least I'm getting mail.
Here where I'm in jail.
And I'll rarely wail.
Except when I feel hail.

For I know it's self-imposed
And were I so disposed
I could leave here unopposed
From this place where I have posed.

As a chained dog I have sat
Wearing a stupid hat
But I'm going to the mat
For dogs and that is that.

So pass SB1435
While the dogs are still alive
Forget about all this jive
Let hope for dogs survive!

—Anonymous.
Ok, it was me.

Random thoughts for the day:

1. Joe is coming up today, but he likes to surprise me. I like surprises, but I really want to know when he's getting here more!

2. I need to start videotaping people's enthusiasm for this law. Cool stuff; this morning I had two awesome reactions, and I never got it on film. You can ask them to repeat it, but then the enthusiasm is forced.

3. As I sit here, I visualize myself connecting with the heroes I'm most inspired by, among the greatest ever. Alice Paul, the suffragist, for her endless determination and single-mindedness. Mother Teresa (I saw Time Magazine put out a special magazine about her, I bought it tonight) for her infinite love for others. Gandhi, for his steadfast determination to right social wrongs. Nelson Mandela for his long-suffering patience and vision in the face of darkness. And Jesus, for his ultimate sacrifice on behalf of those he loved. Drawing from their amazing strength helps get me through.

4. Weatherwise, it's been the best week yet. Only a few sprinkles here and there, not overly hot or cold. I've come to realize how many days of the year chained dogs suffer due to weather here in Pennsylvania on top of the lack of food, water, physical care, and socialization with humans. There are a lot of them.

5. The French tours continue to come by and sympathize with the plight of American dogs. Really, do we want our country known as such blatant animal abusers? I think not.

Day 20
200 Hours on a Chain

August 27

Former foster Sweet Pea comes to visit with Mom Cherie and Justin

I know I shouldn't feel guilty that I'm looking forward to my weekend. But somehow in the last 20 days, I've taken on the pain of the chained dog in a whole new way.

I've spent time on a chain at Chain Offs annually, doing as much as 33 hour the first two years, and through that gained a greater understanding of the plight of the chained dog.

After spending 20 days chained at the Capitol, it's become so much less about who I am as a person and so much more about how can I make the most difference for them.

How can I become a more effective advocate for these dogs that have no voice? How can I set aside my own personal short-comings and feelings of inadequacy and stand up to lead the way to a brighter future for chained dogs?

I believe every human has a mission in life—a mission that is so pure it can only come from God or the universe. One has but to seek and it will be revealed to you.

I've had Christians say to me, "If only you put the passion into spreading the gospel that you put into saving these dogs, you would be a force to be reckoned with." As if what I'm doing is somehow less-than.

I believe that is flawed logic. God doesn't have only one single mission on this planet. A passion this strong and this right can only come from a power greater than myself, a source of strength that goes beyond the every day.

There are thousands or even millions of missions available to us as humans, and when we connect with the energy of God or whatever force you feel guides the universe, we cannot help but come away with a task that is daunting yet so fulfilling in its pursuit.

I spent two years seeking my mission. Each time I questioned God as to what it could possibly be, a picture of the dog named Worthless up the road materialized in my head.

Worthless was a plain old black lab, a gentle dog who wanted only love, a soft bed, and a kind word with his food and water. He was chained to a pole and was often tangled around a nearby tree. My complaints to the humane officer only netted him a worse existence, chained at the bottom of the hill in the mud and ice.

I became obsessed with his well-being, and as I drove by him each day, I would mutter to myself "dogs deserve better."

Yet I told God repeatedly that I was sorry, that mission was too hard for me. I needed an easier mission.

I was to discover that missions have a life of their own, and Worthless' plight could not be denied. I was called to help him.

Eight years later, as I ruminate on Day 20 and the 200 hours I've spent here at the Pennsylvania Capitol of Harrisburg on their behalf—only 1/481 of the time most dogs spend chained in a lifetime—I feel a greater force at work for them.

We as a people must take a stronger stand against the chaining and abuse of dogs. We must rise to the challenge and allow this force to work through us for the betterment of dogs. Keeping Man's Best Friend cruelly chained for life amounts to nothing less than tyranny. And as Thomas Jefferson said "Resistance to tyrants is obedience to God."

Miscellaneous stuff from today:

1. A state rep sent a cafeteria lady down to get my lunch order. I explained that I was fasting until 6:00 p.m., but that I would take a pretzel and an unsweetened iced tea, and eat the pretzel later. At 3:00 someone brought down three pretzels and two iced teas. I'm not sure who the rep was, and the woman didn't know either, so I wanted to say a thank you from here! Your kindness was appreciated. I would gladly thank you in person if I knew who you were.

2. I have a 10:00 meeting Monday morning with Mike Brubaker's aide Kristin Crawford. Brubaker is the head of the Ag Committee, where our bill is stalled, so we'll see how the meeting goes. I'm assuming I will have to meet her at her office inside the Capitol, so I'm hoping maybe a couple of my friends can cover my spot while I go meet for 15 minutes?

3. It was the cutest thing! Lori McGowan and her daughter Emily, with her two friends Victoria and Alexa Marshall came by my spot, brought me a great hat that says 'Woof,' iced tea, and a piece of cake for later. The girls brought two violins and a cello,

and played music for us. They had to compete with the preachers bellowing across the street and the cars honking for Deb Smith's "Honk to Free Chain Dogs" sign, but it was all SO much more entertainment than most chained dogs get in a week!

4. Cherie Smith and Justin Strawser visited in the late afternoon, with my old foster dog Sweet Pea and her sister Lacey. We laughed so hard because Lacey kept dropping logs wherever she sat, which usually happened to be right by my feet. We think she was sending a message to the Capitol about her thoughts on chaining dogs.

I said she was laying eggs. She'd look like she was sitting, then get up and move, and there would be a turd egg. Only dog people find poop funny. It's either laugh or cry, people!

5. I only got one letter today…I'm suspicious I had more, but who knows where they were. The one I did receive was opened and came 'by way of the governor's office.' Well, it had a grand tour anyway! Thanks to Gillian Phillips of New York for taking us to the governor! Total letters: 14.

Day 21
21 Was Not my Lucky Number

August 30

☯☯

I get my mailbox affixed to the side of my house, with two of our stickers on it. Cool.

Today I think I had the beginnings of heat exhaustion. I got a headache and became nauseous and dizzy, but luckily Cathie saved me by bringing iced tea and spelling me for a break while I got some Juicy Rumors fresh juice. The feeling passed.

This was only Day 1 of this week's forecasted 4-day heat spell, and tomorrow's supposed to be in the mid-nineties. It was scary because I can't help but think if I collapse out there there's a good chance no one would even notice or get me help.

At 10:00 a.m. Mary Jo McClain and I met with Senator Brubaker's aide Kristin Crawford. (Brubaker's head of the Ag Committee, where our bill is languishing.) I wish I could say this was a meeting with a positive outcome, but it was my distinct impression that 21 days on a chain was not enough to convince them of the efficacy of this bill.

I wonder if any of them even took a look at the way I'm living out there, and thought for one second how these dogs live like this every single day, all day long? All year long? All lifetime long?

The biggest problem for them appears to be the fact that the bill has a time limit. *How inconvenient for your average chainer! Can we do something about that?*

Apparently the fact that we've already compromised ourselves out of 2/3 of the freedom that a chained dog deserves still isn't enough. We heard the old, tired argument that these things are already covered under the existing cruelty laws. **Bull.**

I challenge you to try to get help for a nearby chained dog, and you'll see that 9.9 times out of ten there is no help forthcoming for them; you will continue to suffer watching them as they continue to suffer living chained.

Mary Jo is very knowledgeable about all aspects of the bill and why each aspect was chosen, in order to compromise with the most people and still provide the dogs with some relief.

My knowledge base is more related to laws in other states and counties, as well as attacks on children and some of the humane cases and why they point to the need for a law. Together I felt we provided a compelling argument for why this bill needs to be pushed forward, and why it needs to be passed before the end of this legislative session.

Although I wish people understood that dogs DO deserve better, I remain undeterred by the current stance. If you, like me, KNOW in your gut that DOGS DESERVE BETTER than life on a chain, please make your voices heard, Pennsylvania! Don't back down. This is not the time to back down.

Miscellaneous trivia from the day:

1. Terry covered me for the meeting, for which I want to thank her. She spent an hour and fifteen minutes chained, and was already roasting when I got back out.

2. The three main people who normally provide me breaks throughout the day were mostly unavailable. Stacey had to take foster kitties to the vet, Melissa didn't work today, and Cathie had meetings, although she did spell me once and brought me drinks twice, thank goodness. I did have water with me just in case anyway, but bathroom breaks were not easy to come by.

3. I wonder if Hurricane Earl will affect Harrisburg…which is worse, four days of 95 degree weather or a tropical storm? That's a tough one.

Day 22
It's a "No-brainer"

August 31

A huge container of ice sits by my ankle and provides a tiny bit of coolness

Why is it that most people in America, and nearly all people in England, France, Germany, Austria, and Switzerland call a law against chaining dogs a "no-brainer?"

Could it be because it's a "no-brainer?"

I know California is advanced, or more 'liberal' as most of the country would say, yet they passed a law limiting chaining to THREE HOURS a day THE FIRST YEAR THEY TRIED. In fact, this issue was chosen by an animal coalition specifically because it was the most likely to get passed. Why? **Because it's a—SAY IT WITH ME—"no-brainer."**

It would be brainless of me to call those I'm trying to solicit a law from brainless, and I wouldn't dream of doing such a thing, but really, six years? SIX YEARS? And they still tell me we have little hope of getting it passed this year?

Come on.

Yesterday we were thanked for exempting the farmers from the bill, and to be perfectly honest, we all know that's only done because their lobby is so strong. Not because farm dogs deserve to be chained.

I've learned that when you're working for a law you make compromises that Christ wouldn't want to make. They don't go down easy.

So, let's review: Your farmers are exempt, and we've given up 2/3 of the time that a dog deserves to be free. And yet you want more?

There's no more left to give.

I heard from one woman with a working farm dog who agreed but was worried that the law would impact her. She told me that her dog lives to herd the sheep. He thrives on it, and requires very little human interaction because he is intense about his job. The ONLY time he is tethered is when a new sheep is introduced, and only until he understands that this particular sheep is part of his herd so he doesn't kill the sheep.

Her dog is working, doing what he yearns to do. He's not chained up on the pretense of being a working farm dog, he's active and fulfilled. I assured her she'd be fine.

I live near a farmer with a working farm dog, a chocolate lab that can be seen daily either riding on the tractor or running along beside his caretaker in the fields. Now THAT is a happy and loved farm dog.

Most farmers who know the value of a dog rarely chain their dogs anyway. Those who use the dog as a cheap alarm system learn to ignore his barks because he barks at animals, people, thunder storms, and sometimes even the wind. The alarm system is ineffective.

I grew up on a farm. I saw horrible deaths befall many an animal, including my father killing all our cats because my mother complained they were trying to come in the house. I also was subject to the daily sight of our beagle, Maggie, chained and languishing at her doghouse.

Maggie was supposedly a hunting dog, but she never got trained, and the one time my brother did take her hunting he lost her in the woods, never to be seen by us again. God knows what fate befell her.

I'm sure we'd have been exempt from the law.

Then I grew up. I realized that just because my family chained our dog didn't make it right. It was wrong, and they've learned enough now to realize it was wrong too.

In fact, most of those who used to chain their dogs wouldn't do it now, but there are still those who really need a law to learn the difference between right and wrong.

Just because so and so has always chained his dogs, and his father before him chained his dogs, doesn't make it right. It's time for America to grow up.

We've compromised all we can compromise. We have given all we can give. I'm here for their law, and I call on all those who love their dogs to LET PENNSYLVANIA KNOW YOU ARE WATCHING THEM.

Europe, California, dog advocates nationwide, TELL PENN-

SYLVANIA NO MORE. There's a woman sitting on your door-step who has had enough, and you have had enough.

Stop the bullshit excuses and give us our law. That's why we're here.

It really is a no-brainer.

Various and sundry daily stuff:

1. Second day in a row of mid-nineties heat. It's still supposed to be as hot through Thursday. I cried this morning when I woke up, because I just didn't know how I could survive the day. I got lucky and finally figured out that there's a tiny patch of shade in the little stairwell that my chain reaches until 1:00 p.m., so then I only have two hours until the shade again reaches that stairwell. During the time there's no shade, I have to stand at the pillar to get just a little bit, which is hard on my ankle.

2. Today Cathie brought me a big cheesy-poof container filled with ice, which I used to cool myself down. I felt a little guilty because I know the dogs don't have such 'luxuries,' but I enjoyed it anyway.

3. A 15-year-old girl and her mom came up to meet me, and her mom said they are talking about my chaining more than their shoes at her school…so I guess that's a good thing!

Day 23
Yes, Mike, I Am a Veteran

September 1

ꙮ

Rep Coordinator Marie Belanger sent me flowers! How beautiful.

His response was "No, it's really not the same. Then people wouldn't have to see some crazy lady chained to a doghouse."

He'd been writing me through Facebook all day long. Now, I normally don't tolerate being annoyed through my Facebook page, and I'll block someone in a heartbeat if they feel a need to come through there and send me hate mail. My personal page is a safe haven for me…you can send DDB hate mail through our fan page or our e-mail if you feel a burning need, but I don't deal with it in my personal space.

However, he hadn't been overly aggressive, and I was feeling bored in the 95 degree heat, so I went ahead and responded briefly to his taunts.

He had asked me, in the rather odd logic that some men show and I clearly don't grasp, why I wasn't chained out at the Capitol from 10 p.m. to 6 a.m. if that was the time period I wanted chaining banned. I said, "What's the difference when I sit out there? Don't the dogs suffer the same at 10 p.m. as they do at 10 a.m.?" I'm there to illustrate their current suffering, and would stay 24/7 if it was allowed and I felt at all safe there. (Which I don't.)

Which is when he replied, **"No, it's really not the same. Then people wouldn't have to see some crazy lady chained to a doghouse."**

Ah, so I'm getting to him! I like it.

When I strolled nonchalantly by Mike's Facebook page that evening, I saw that he was a big military guy, in the Army, and a youngster, graduating in '09. Clearly, he knew it all and he wasn't afraid to use it.

That's when I pulled out the weapon that shut him up and sent him scurrying back to the darkness from whence he came; yes, *Mike, I too am a military girl—so am I still just some crazy lady chained to a doghouse?*

When I served in the USAF at the tender age of 20-25, I did it for many reasons…adventure, dedication to my country, schooling, and escape from the backwoods of Pennsylvania. I did well in the Air Force, made Staff Sergeant at first opportunity, got honors in my Czech linguist studies, and met people who I would always consider my family. I was honorably discharged in November,

1988, went back to college, and joined the workforce.

I was lucky to never end up in a war zone, and I don't know how I would have turned out if I had seen combat.

I spoke to one of our supporters from my area who was both Air Force and then National Guard, ending up in Iraq for a 12-month assignment. He described to me how terrifying it was watching people get destroyed in Iraq, and then coming home to nothing even close to resembling a hero's welcome. He hasn't been the same since.

In Tyson's honor, I want to personally extend my thanks to all our troops who endured Operation Iraqi Freedom and survived. I pray you can find peace upon your return home, and my heart goes out to you for all the suffering you've endured.

I would think someone like Mike, who fights for the freedom of America, would **understand why a veteran would find freedom so necessary that she would fight for freedom for Man's Best Friend.**

You might say dogs aren't people, and I would agree with that. Dogs are much more forgiving, much more loving, and much more needy than people.

And, they can't fight for themselves.

So forgive me, Mike, and any other military member who thinks chaining our best friends for life is OK, if I disagree with you and tell you that you might want to **go back and take another look at the definition of freedom.**

There are other freedoms worth fighting for, and dogs have served our country—have indeed given their lives—for America. Now it's our turn to do this just and right thing for them. Don't you think we owe them that much?

I do.

Day 24
I Hit the Wall Today

September 2

On the bright side, I was losing weight...was being the operative word.

I don't know what to tell you. I hit the wall today, and although I didn't leave and didn't even consider leaving (sorry, Senators) **I just huddled up in a ball and cried.**

One of the Fido's Freedom supporters (Abbie Withers) wrote this on the wall: "Tamira....I want you to tell the world how it feels sitting there endlessly in the hot sun....every time you feel overheated, hungry, thirsty, weary, scared, bored, unloved, trapped...tell us every detail....then tell it again and again until someone hears you."

I replied back, "I'd be saying that every second then."

Of course I feel those things every day, but I can't put all that whining onto you. It's my job to be strong out here, and today I failed in that job.

I felt like I failed the dogs, and I failed myself, because my human insecurities got the better of me.

I can't MAKE these lawmakers do the right thing. I can't MAKE Senator Brubaker lead the Ag Committee into getting this bill to the floor for a vote. I can't make them care.

These dogs depend on me, and *many of the lawmakers could give a shit less.*

This week I survived four days of absolute HELL heat. Both today and yesterday the thermometer hit 99 degrees. As I sat there, huddled on the steps with only my feet in a tiny patch of shade, I laid my head on my knees and I wept.

I wept for the dogs, and I wept for me. I wept for all those who are suffering and who will not receive the help they need today, and for all the kind-hearted neighbors who are forced to watch the suffering dogs with no relief from the abuse.

I wept for those who hold power and use it only for their own greed and self-aggrandizement. I wept for the world they destroy and the lives they brutalize.

I wept in despair and I wept in sadness, a sadness that clings to me still at this very moment.

The cards you all sent me cheered me on, and some of the things you said blew me away.

Like this from Pamela Presley: **"We hope—all of us who are advocates and all of them sitting at the end of a chain—**

hope you stay strong and that your fight, our fight, will bring change."

Although I am down, I will not stay down. Although I am lost, I will again find my way. And although I am weak, I will again grow strong. Please continue your fight with me. Keep making those phone calls, which we've heard have come from all over the world to the PA state senators. Most of all, ask your Pennsylvania friends to stand up for chained dogs. They cannot stand up for themselves.

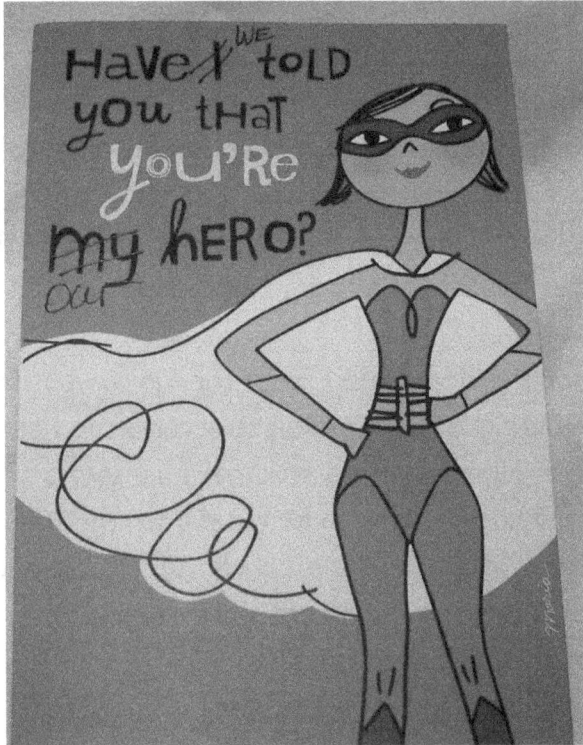

One of the cards that cheered me up considerably.

Day 25
What A Long, Hard Week it's Been

September 3

☯

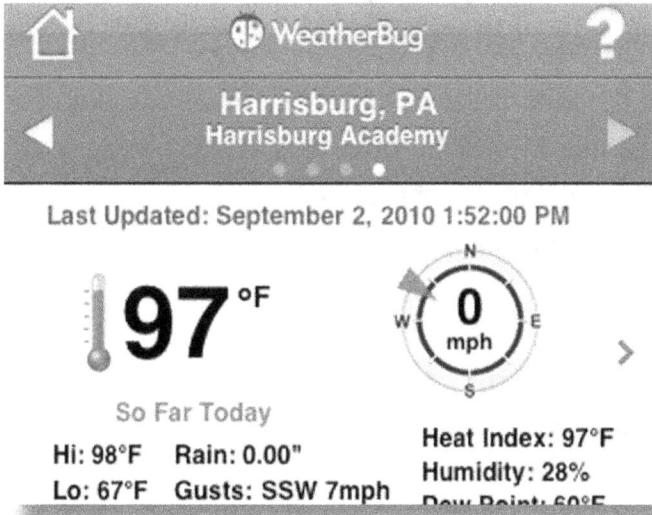

Last Updated: September 2, 2010 1:52:00 PM

97 °F

Harrisburg, PA
Harrisburg Academy

WeatherBug

0 mph

So Far Today

Hi: 98°F   Rain: 0.00"
Lo: 67°F   Gusts: SSW 7mph

Heat Index: 97°F
Humidity: 28%
Dew Point: 60°F

A screen capture from one of the hottest temperature reads of the week. Killer!

My good friend, DDB cohort, author and illustrator of the up-coming "A New Name for Worthless," Rocky Shepheard, came to spend the afternoon with me.

We spent 5 hours sitting on the steps together, during which time the temp hit 90—the lowest of the week—and I still had rivulets of sweat pouring down my back (I always wanted to use that word in a sentence. Finally!) Rocky mentioned repeatedly that he was roasting to death, to which I'd say, "Well, it's not like it was yesterday. Or the day before that. Or that..."

When the end of the day finally came, we walked back to the parking garage to pick up our vehicles, and he said "F@*k! I'm glad I don't have to do that again."

I burst out laughing.

He always does make me laugh.

He said "You must be a really strong woman."

I rarely see myself as strong. I think I'm too weak, and so much of the time I just want to say screw it and walk away from everything. I want to go play on a deserted island with Joe and never worry about dog rescue or who is torturing their dog this week, or how am I going to save this dog or get this law passed.

I'm tired, I'm exhausted, and I'm mentally drained. I'm frustrated, angry, sad, and hurt. I'm a mixed up, damaged, flawed woman, but I'm also one who picks herself back up, dusts herself off, and goes again despite all those who want her to go away.

I want this bill to pass because these dogs deserve this right and just act. I want this bill to pass because I want every dog to know the freedom and joy that the dogs DDB's rescued have known.

136

I want this bill to pass because there's no such dog as an 'outside dog.' There's labs, there's beagles, there's Akitas, and there's spaniels who look exactly like the lab, beagle, Akita, and spaniel living inside with their pack just down the street. There is no genetic difference, only a difference in treatment by Americans who are too [fill in the blank] to learn to do better.

I watched Miss Sugar run in the stream in the woods near my house. I watched her frolic to and fro through a mud puddle until she was thoroughly covered, and then she turned around and did it again. When she saw I was watching, she ran up to me for approval as if to say "Did you like what I did, Mommy?"

I said "Yes, I do sweetie. I love what you did, and you keep doing it every chance you get because with every spark of life and playful step you heal my heart."

Day 26
The Doghouse Goes Mobile!

September 6

☙❧

Deb Smith and Tami chained at the Kipona Festival

Today we took the doghouse mobile, going down by the river to the Kipona Festival because it was Labor Day. We spent several hours chained there, divvying up chaining time between myself, Joe, Deb Smith, and Mike and Stacey Romberger. In doing so we were seen by at least 1000 people, so it was definitely the wiser choice than sitting at the Capitol by myself. Quite a few stopped by to ask questions, and we planted seeds in many minds.

Remember, I will be doing a four day fast and silent vigil for chained dogs September 7-10 while chained to my doghouse in Harrisburg, PA. Please join me in whatever way works for you... silence, prayer, meditation, fasting...let's bring the divine to this mission, and save these chained dogs!

I will be cutting off all internet communications for the four days, so please continue to spread the word in my place.

WOMAN UNDERTAKES 4-DAY SILENT FAST WHILE CHAINED TO DOGHOUSE ON HARRISBURG CAPITOL STEPS

VIGIL FOR LAW FOR CHAINED DOGS REACHES 250 HOURS

Tamira Thayne, founder of the anti-chaining nonprofit organization Dogs Deserve Better, has spent 25 days—250 hours—chained to a doghouse in front of the State Capitol Building in Harrisburg, Pennsylvania, to pass SB1435, a law which would help chained dogs.

On Day 26, Labor Day, Thayne plans to go mobile with her doghouse to reach Kipona crowds, a huge riverfront festival lasting all weekend, since the state Capitol will be quiet.

Then she will spend four days in a silent vigil and fast while chained to her doghouse at the Capitol steps. She has daily blogged, twittered, and facebooked from her chain, but internet communications, as well as speech and all food and drink except water will be cut off during those four days.

"I feel we need a spark of the divine in this mission," Thayne explains, adding that she really wants to focus her energies on bringing some Higher Help for Pennsylvania's 'Forgotten' dogs.

"Every session we fail to get legislative help for chained and abused dogs is another two years of hell they must endure. I believe that God sent me on this mission to bring help for Man's Best Friend, and I'm asking all dog lovers in Pennsylvania to join me in silence, prayer, meditation, or fasting so resolution can come quickly for these helpless creatures."

Thayne is fed up with Pennsylvania's stance when it comes to a law limiting the suffering of both the chained dogs and caring neighbors who are forced to watch the abuse without any recourse. She knows people who have moved just so they don't have to watch the suffering any longer, and questions why those who abuse their dogs have more rights than the caring neighbor next door?

She quotes a supporter, Samantha Devine, who wrote, "Why lawmakers would not pass such a law is beyond me; either they care so little as to be considered heartless or wish to appease the lowest of humanity, for no person who has known the love of a pet would willingly allow such cruelty to continue."

Thayne hopes that Pennsylvania dog lovers will continue to call members of the Senate Ag Committee during her vigil, and make plans to attend a dog rally on the steps of the Capitol September 13, 2010, from 11:00 a.m. to 1:00 p.m. in support of anti-chaining legislation, the gas chamber bill, and puppy mill laws.

She also asks supporters to attend Mike Brubaker's town hall meeting with her September 15, 2010, from 6:30-8:00 p.m. to urge him to allow the bill out of the Ag Committee so it may go to the Senate Floor for a vote.

Days 27-30
Undertaking a Silent Vigil and Fast

September 7-10

&G;

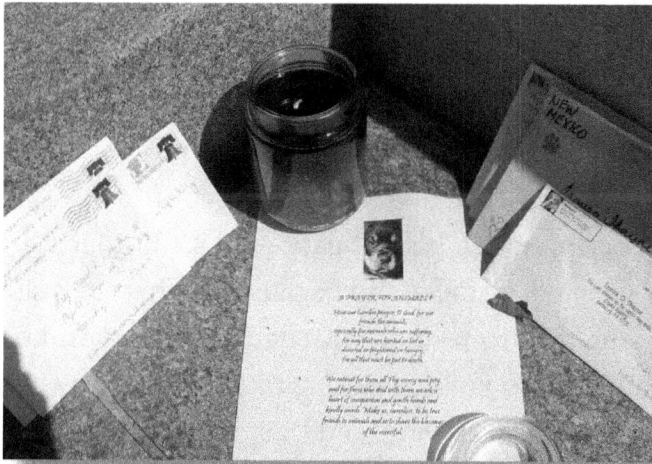

Letters of support, with a candle and prayer from friend Cathie MacArthur

The chained dogs have no voice, and for four days neither did I. These dogs rely on us, and now I have an even greater understanding of why they need to.

We are more important to them than we can possibly understand.

I am one of the loudest voices for chained dogs…with me silenced for four days, I have to ask—did you speak for me? For them? Did you spread the word, ask others to call their senators, make plans to attend the rally on the 13th or Mike Brubaker's town hall meeting on the 15th?

The internet can be our best friend or our worst enemy. It has enabled us to spread the news worldwide and instantly, yet has given people the false sense that they are being active when they haven't left the computer desk.

Making time in my life to chain myself at the Capitol was an excruciating process. Not only did I have my plate full with everyday DDB tasks and campaigns—some of which is my own armchair activism—but I had speaking engagements lined up, events planned, and I wanted time to play with my family and dogs and cats.

I knew I would have to give up most everything for months, find a way to squeeze in absolutely necessary work and my loved ones, and somehow still find time to sleep.

I was afraid to do it, and kept putting it off.

It's not convenient. It's not easy. And it's not fun.

Fasting so much stinks, and because my thyroid is sluggish and I'm too stubborn to take any but natural remedies, I barely lose weight anyway, so am not getting much in the way of side benefits. I feel like I'm starving, and I get sick from not eating, but I know the dogs are lucky if they get one meal per day. So I stick it out.

And who's idea was it to do a silent vigil, anyway? I initially though I might like it, because I'm an introvert, but mostly it was just annoying and exhausting.

So what did I gain from a 4-day silent vigil? Besides the desire to never partake of one again?

A better understanding of the amount of helplessness felt by the chained dog. Not only are they unable to make their needs known *(I'm ever more floored by the nerve of chainers to tell me—*

and delude themselves that it's true—that these dogs LIKE it out on the chain) but they are increasingly more frustrated by the effort to communicate with their human caregivers.

I also gained understanding of how a vigil brings spiritual power to a cause. I felt strongly that our campaign needed to touch the divine, to reach a place where barriers are exploded and so are the chains man has shackled our best friends to.

By being silent for four days, I was able to keep my energy focused inward, to pull in more God-strength, and become more of a channel for the power of the Divine.

I'll be the first to say I'm not outwardly religious these days, although I've always been very spiritual, and carry a deep belief in the effects of this power in our lives.

I wrote a prayer for chained dogs, which I used as a basis for spiritual interaction daily around 8 a.m., noon, and 4 p.m. I read it repeatedly to myself, and I felt the energy of the prayer swirl through me, felt it's force.

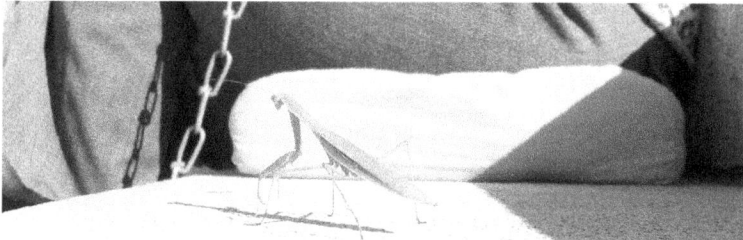

Through these efforts, I drew to myself a praying mantis (get it?—literally, he landed on my back and then sat with me for 1/2 hour), a nice young man who wanted to pray together, and numerous interviews and media attention even while silent.

From these days of silence I learned just how valuable is my ability to speak. My voice is a treasure that I must use as much as possible on behalf of chained dogs, and other who are suffering. Your voice is equally as valuable. Please use it now to let the PA senators know that chaining is unacceptable.

Our Prayer for Chained Dogs

Dear God,
We bring to your our voiceless,
Our sad, our lonely,
Our chained.

And ask that you will
Scoop them up
Into the arms of
The Divine.

Comforting them, protecting them,
Calming them.
Breaking the chains
Man has bound them to.

Free them with
A Love so Powerful
It shatters all barriers
Destroys all opposition

And knows the Truth:
Dogs DO Deserve Better

Tamira Ci Thayne, September 7, 2010

Day 31
Rally for Animal Laws at the Capitol

September 13

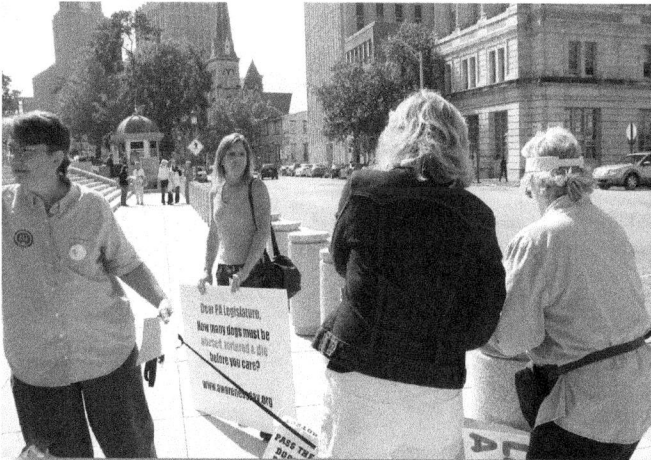

DDB and other animal supporters prepare for the rally

A rally for all pending animal bills awaiting passage was held on the Capitol steps today. I was scheduled to speak, so Mike helped me carry my doghouse up the steps where I spoke from my chain, dragging it along behind me to the podium.

Video of my speech may be viewed at the following YouTube link: http://youtu.be/8r-n082tGys.

When I walked up to the mic I said to everyone: "Welcome to my neighborhood." Although I guess I lived in the ghetto, at the bottom of the steps instead of at the top!

A total of about 100 people came out, some with dogs, but the attendance looked poorer due to the heat, with everyone sitting over in the grass instead of congregating around the speakers.

Any day that included something out of the ordinary was a good day for me, and seeing supporters who were proud of me and what I was trying to do for chained dogs lifted my spirits considerably.

Day 32
Cruelty to Humans

September 14

☙❧

I'm still bigger than the Capitol building, I told you so.

When states, cities, or counties balk at adding chaining laws, it's always, in one way or another, related to "property" rights.

Dogs are property.

Since dogs are nothing but more lawn garbage for a certain segment of the population, they think nothing of chaining them to trees to rot for their entire lives. It's perfectly legal.

The dogs may start with a nice, lightweight chain, but after they have the unmitigated gall to break that chain in an attempt to get to the humans they so long to be near, the chain becomes progressively thicker until they're dragging a 50-lb. tow chain.

I've seen it many times.

Our society's "look the other way" mentality allows this abuse to go on out of a misguided fear of curtailing the rights of "property" owners.

Yet this failure to provide protection for dogs does a lot more than protect those who neglect animals; it inflicts cruelty to humans.

That's right. By legislators failing to pass a bill limiting chaining, they sentence not only dogs to a life of hell, but **the humans who witness the suffering to prolonged emotional abuse.**

I was recently speaking to a woman who wanted to buy a home in a small town in Ohio. The house she wanted to buy was exactly what she was looking for, with a big, privacy-fenced yard, but she could hear a dog barking in the yard next door. She looked through the slats to see a dog chained in the neighbor's yard, barking for attention and looking in her direction, wagging his tail.

She made her decision immediately, telling the realtor there was no way she'd buy that house, as she'd probably end up arrested before all was said and done for decking the neighbor.

A businessman I met moved from New Jersey to North Carolina to enjoy a restful retirement. Instead he ended up charged with disturbing the peace because he couldn't stop tangling with his neighbor over having to watch their dog suffer in the backyard. Last I talked to him he was moving away just to get away from the pain of watching that dog.

The pain of watching a black lab near me—Worthless was

his name (believe it or not)—suffer for six years **drove me to form Dogs Deserve Better.** I wanted to move away to flee my own pain of seeing him standing in the mud and ice, but I figured there'd just be another dog chained nearby wherever I moved.

I am not alone. **Caring citizens in our country deserve better than to suffer emotional bondage right along with the suffering chained dog next door.** I regularly get calls from people who cry in helplessness because of a dog chained near them. They describe the dog to me, love for a creature who doesn't even "belong" to them evident in their voices. My heart breaks for them.

They've tried everything—speaking to the caretaker, sending DDB information, getting the humane officer to visit, even calling the police. Nothing has worked.

They are in so much pain, many of them cannot sleep at night, they toss and turn with worry about the dog's welfare. Does he have water? Has he eaten today? Will he be alive in the morning?

Do not these people have rights too? Do they not have the right to be free of the emotional turmoil of watching man's best friend in jeopardy?

Will we continue to protect the rights of those who show regard neither for canine nor human suffering over the rights of the victims?

We can take a step toward ending it here in Pennsylvania by passing anti-tethering legislation. Do not be fooled by those who chain their dogs for life yet claim to "love" them. Love does not do harm to another.

Pass this bill and **end the cruelty to humans. Oh, and dogs too.**

Miscellaneous observations of the day:

1. There is this one guy who wonders the streets a lot, and he's usually carrying a bible and a tambourine. I don't know what his deal is, but he seems harmless enough. He talks kinda' effeminately, and is usually quite gregarious. I found out he was a veteran when he gave me a flyer about buying houses. Yesterday he walked by and just looked down and very sad, didn't say a word. Not like him.

About 1/2 hour later there were three cop cars, with two plain clothes police and two uniformed police surrounding him, and he had changed into an old army uniform. I'm not sure what was going on, but he must have done something violent to have them surround him like that. I missed what happened in the end, though, and didn't see if they took him into custody or not.

2. People sneak pictures of me all the time instead of openly taking them or asking if they can take one. It's kinda' weird. If people take pics and put them on their Facebook, it spreads the word, so I don't care if they do. I don't think there can be a worse picture of me than the one in the Patriot last week. I thought the Altoona Mirror won the prize with their "Criminal" pic of me, but the one last week was hideous. Thanks, Patriot! When you take fifty pics you can't tell me there's not a decent one or two in there? Even Joe, who tries to be so supportive, was like, um, honey…yeah…well, I guess he can be happy the men aren't all over me with that pic floating around! I looked like Squidward from Spongebob. No shit.

3. The angry couple have moved their pickup spot down the street. I wonder if they read the blog? Well, they were annoying anyway. I'm sure they're still not interacting well wherever they are. I vote for counseling.

Day 33
Mike Brubaker: A Good Time was Had by All

September 15

⚭

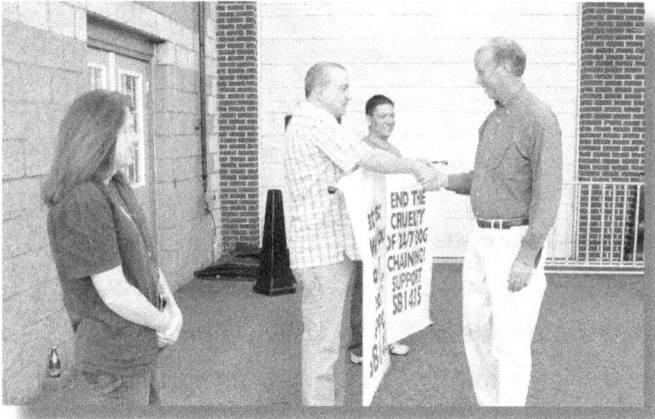

Brubaker (right) greets DDB supporters

Well, I've gotta hand it to him…Mike Brubaker is a consummate politician. He treated us with courtesy and respect at the town hall meeting (well, all but Gordon, who went first and ruffled his feathers a bit), all the while refusing to say that he supports the bill.

He told us the usual stuff…that there simply wasn't enough time in the session to get anywhere with our bill. Pulled out the "there's 4000 bills that come through our legislature each year, only 10% of which get passed…and that's the way it should be."

The implication here is that perhaps our bill just isn't one of the 10%, or there's not enough time to explore whether it can make the cut or not. **But we all KNOW it is...so what are we going to do about it?** Are we going to sit here and cry in our cornflakes, or are we going to let them know just how serious we are about dogs and chains?

What will you do to show the senators how serious you are about passing a bill for chained dogs? You know what I'm doing. Will you stand beside me, figuratively, if not literally?

Brubaker is definitely key to getting this bill out of committee, and he as much as said it's his job to vet the bills. Well, it's also his job to do what the majority of Pennsylvanians want.... and haven't we all let him know what we want? Have you?

If you haven't, I need you to go up to the nearest chained dog and tell him or her you're sorry; that you were too busy doing [insert excuse here] to take time to stand up for them, and they will just have to wait another two years until maybe someone decides it's time for PA to stop being so cruelty-ridden.

Let's hope they survive that long.

I can't do this alone...and I need YOU to step up and help me. That's the bottom line.

We had around 15 supporters show up for the meeting, not bad considering we filled half the room. He gave us a block of time at 7:00, and we spoke until 7:45.

At least eight of us spoke up, and everyone was very passionate and caring. I think we did great, and I'm incredibly happy and grateful for those of you who came and made a difference. *Thank you. It meant a lot to me and the dogs.*

Key points I brought up to Brubaker:

I know that you were instrumental in getting the puppymill legislation passed, and as a dog lover, I thank you.

In your newsletter you stated "I am proud that we've been able to ensure more humane treatment for animals that will someday serve as our beloved family pets." But see, that's the problem...there's all too many that are not beloved family pets, who will languish and die without ever knowing anything but life at the end of a chain. A chained dog who spends eleven years chained before dying will spend 96,000 hours chained.

96,000 hours.

Last night Harrisburg city council passed a resolution requesting the Senate to pass SB1435. It passed by a vote of 7-0. I spoke to Animal Control officer Fred Lamke about it, and his response was "It's about time."

You are quoted in the Pittsburgh Tribune-Review as saying "There's nothing wrong with tethering in and of itself."

Yet chained dogs are three times more likely to bite according to the Center for Disease Control. The absolute highest bite factor comes from a chained, unneutered, male dog.

In the month and a half since I've been at the Capitol, there have been three chained dog attacks on children that made the news. Two-year-old Molina Reyes in Philly, an unidentified eleven-year-old near Pittsburgh, and six-year-old Alaha Crutchfield, who was nearly scalped by a chained dog. She's lucky to be alive.

So when you say chaining isn't bad in and of itself, I would say these children would disagree. I also wonder how the mother of Brianna Shanor, who died from a chained dog attack last January, would feel about that statement.

The humans who have to suffer as they watch the neighbor's dog pace frantically each and every day, knowing there's nothing they can do to help the dog would also emphatically disagree.

And let's not forget the dogs themselves, who spend on average 96,000 hours on a chain. If they could speak, what would they say?

I've just spent 330 hours chained out there, and it's been absolutely miserable, so I feel I'm the one most qualified at this point to speak on their behalf. They vote NO to tethering.

If you want to make life better for man's best friend, passing SB1435 is one step in that direction. **If you say you're for more humane treatment of dogs, now's your chance to prove it.**

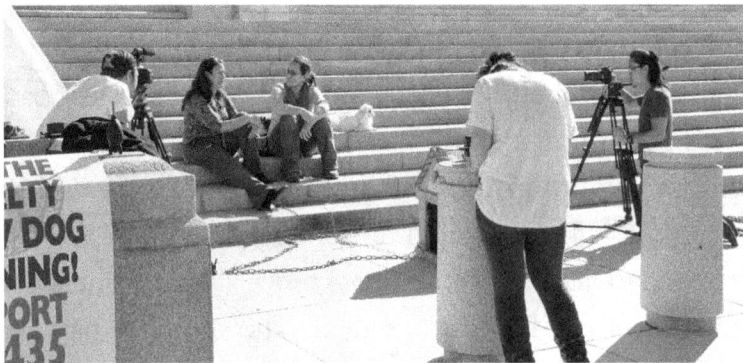

Film student Lorena De Miranda Marques spends the day filming for her project

Day 34
Fell Over from Exhaustion

September 16

Afternoon in the rain and radio show with idiots, what a day!

Day 34 brought a few more negative events into my life as a chained dog. The first was that we had an afternoon of soaking rain, which at the time I knew I really couldn't complain about—we've been in a drought, which has been bad for the crops and Pennsylvania in general, but good for the lady chained at the Capitol.

We needed the rain.

Still, enduring the four hours of soaking rain is another thing entirely. Taking a potty break when your clothes are stuck to your body and have to be peeled away layer by layer is a struggle to say the least. I know the dogs don't have this issue…they squat or lift their leg somewhere within the radius of their chain out of sheer necessity, but **I am a human with human needs and wearing human clothes and that is not an option for me.**

The temperatures were in the lower 60's, not a freezing rain, but enough to chill me to the bone. I did not sit for the entire four hours because the only dry spot was the top of my pants and under my butt, and I wanted to keep it that way as long as I could.

Not sitting made my ankle sprain flare and the outside of my right ankle was swollen and painful. This made it difficult to walk or even stand.

I was indeed miserable.

My neck has also started to cause me problems, the bones are not lining up right or something, and the ache on the right side of my neck from the weight of the chain every day has increased.

This reminds me of Biddy, a dog rescued by Cynthia Sweet from near me in Blandburg, PA, this winter. She paid the guy $300 just to get the dog out of there…and only had poor Biddy for a short period of time before she ended up having to put him to sleep due to **the bones in his neck being so damaged that they caused him an almost-paralysis and an inability to move without screaming in pain.**

Just one of the effects of chaining your dog for life.

To add to that misery, I went on the Bob Durgin show, which

is really not a good idea if you don't want to get into a Jerry Springer-like brawl with him and his callers who crawl out from under their boulder to tell you how happy their dogs are living out on their chains.

And that THEIR dog loves it outside alone. He or she truly does.

Where do these people come from?

I was lucky that the misery of dealing with Durgin and his callers distracted me from the misery of standing in the rain.

I was also lucky that Joe stood out there with me much of the day. In fact, that boy being a man, he sat down on the wall and even fell asleep sitting in the rain. I don't know how they do it.

I kept trying to get him out of the rain, but he refused, saying he was staying out there with me. I know what it's like for the caring souls who've befriended me out here, and worry about me in the rain and weather the way I worry about the chained dogs near me. I know it must be even harder for Joe, because he loves me very much, to deal with me undergoing the stress that I've put myself under by doing this.

To Joe and all the friends I've made, thank you. You all have been wonderful and caring, and I apologize that I've given you something to worry about. **You all know why I have to do it, for these dogs who have no one to stand up for them, no one to advocate for them, no one to be a voice for them.**

What I was most struck by with Durgin and the yahoos who call into his show is that even if they do not chain their own dog, they don't give a rat's ass about the dogs who are left out there on a chain.

Durgin bragged to me that his dog has never, EVER been on a tether...yet he refuses to support a law which would give other yellow labs just like his eight lousy hours off a chain per day.

How self-centered can you be? Really?

When I got back last night and tried to work in bed on my blog, it just didn't work. I literally ended up falling over in exhaustion, at which point I said, "There's just no way I can do this," snuggled under the covers and went to sleep.

I awoke feeling fragile and extremely sad. Sad that there are such losers in our world who harm dogs and who don't stand in the way of others harming them, and sad that we cannot make our legislature listen to those of us who are willing to stand up. It's a real shame.

Think about it: which group are you in?

Day 35
Guest Blogger Gordon Bakalar

September 17

Gordon Bakalar takes his turn sitting for me

My friend and longtime DDB supporter Gordon Bakalar wrote such a kick-butt letter to Brubaker that I decided to use it as a guest blog today. I also posted a video of my 35 days on a chain, it is viewable at this YouTube link: http://youtu.be/5kQ7wtxZzjc.

Dear Senator Brubaker:

It was good to meet you at the town meeting you so graciously hosted at the fire house in Witmer.

I don't know how much good it will do, but I'd like to get a few concerns off my chest, several of which I may not have addressed at the meeting, and some may be ground already covered. I hope you will bear with me.

I think you avoided the question: "Are you for or against SB1435, the dog tethering bill?" You took no definite stand one way or the other. I think you don't want to be seen as against the well-being of dogs because there are so many dog owners and animal lovers—that would be like being against apple pie or the American flag—un-American.

My opinion, although you say you owned four dogs in your life, and may have "loved" those dogs, I don't believe you have compassion for chained dogs. Compassion is defined as sympathy for a being in stress. To have compassion you must feel in yourself what that other person or animal is feeling.

I believe you, as Chairman of the Agricultural Committee, will just let the bill be debated to a slow death, just like many dogs are chained to a slow death.

If this were a bill that you favored, I think it is in your power to push for an up or down vote just as the bill is written, without debate and without amendments.

Here is how I feel about chained dogs: I have compassion for these dogs. Why? Because I feel dogs that are in the backyard are alone and ignored. They are out of sight, therefore out of mind. If they are a family dog I believe that the responsibility for the dogs care is given to children for training—the experience of taking care of an animal.

But kids forget. So sometimes the dog suffers lack of food, or water, clean up, you name it. And perhaps the care of the dog is shifted from one family member to another and through miscommunication, the dog suffers.

I think the suffering of chained dogs can, in some measure be alleviated by this anti-tethering bill. How? The owner will be forced or have the opportunity to get to know his dog better and be encouraged to train the dog. Health issues will be more likely to be addressed if the owner has to take his dog off the chain, and maybe the dog will get some exercise.

I think the laws regarding animal welfare are maturing, progressing because it is the correct, the just, action to take. As a comparison, slavery was acceptable 200 years or so ago. No longer. Segregation was the norm decades ago. Not any more. Lots of people smoked in their homes, cars, or restaurants not so long ago. Not so much now.

Times are changing. Animal welfare must advance just as those issues I mentioned have. Pennsylvania's animal protection AND enforcement are sadly lacking and way behind many other more enlightened states.

What I believe:

1-I believe all dogs are meant to be companions.

2-I believe all chained dogs suffer by being chained.

3-I believe most chained dogs get tangled in their chains.

4-I believe most chained dogs do not get access to water because the chain spills the bowl

5-I believe many chained dogs miss food and water because someone forgot or was too busy that day; out of sight, out of mind.

6-I believe all chained dogs suffer from the heat of summer and most from the cold of winter, sometimes to the point of death.

7-I believe most chained dogs do not get the vet care they need nor the flea and tick meds they should have and many do not have proper inoculations.

8-I believe most of the time the area around the dog is not cleaned up and the dog is forced to lie in his own feces and mud.

9- I believe in many cases, people say dogs are chained due to economic circumstances. However, it is less expensive to bring a dog into your house and hopefully your heart.

10-I believe not everyone should own a dog.

11-I believe you have no right to own a dog if you have to chain your dog every day of its life with no reprieve. It is torture, cruel and inhumane, to keep a dog chained.

Who Will Speak For Me

No house, no shelter, no home have I
I lie on muddy ground like a pig sty

Tangled and matted is my hair
Eyes clouded over, just a blank stare

I beg for food, anything to eat
At times too weak to stay on my feet

No, I'm no bum. I'm not a person you see
Just a no name dog who's chained to a tree

I used to be a proud Great Dane
Now skin and bones on a six foot chain

Supposedly the family pet
But neither food nor water do I get

Out in heat, out in the cold
Suffering in silence 'til I'm too old

No one hears my howl of pain
As my collar chokes me again and again

No one pays attention to me
'Cause I'm just a piece of property

Enduring a life of unending sorrow
Looking for a friend today…or tomorrow

I have no vote, I have no voice
But passing SB1435 would be my choice

Who will stand and speak for me?
Any one on the Ag committee?

Gordon Bakalar, September 17, 2010

Day 36
Bite the Hand that Feeds You

September 20

Pennsylvania's "Wall of Shame" shows chained dogs in many counties, and was featured at Awareness Day and Woofstock, where 10,000 people saw it.

Today there was a rally on the steps for homelessness, especially those who are released from prison and have nowhere to go. That would be very sad if you were genuinely trying to change your life and yet no one would give you a place to live let alone work, food, and clothing.

Being out here all day every day has given me insight into the homeless issue that I had heretofore not experienced in my generally rural existence.

I can't say I find it enjoyable.

Most suit-types pretend I don't exist or pretend they don't see me, much the way all of society (myself included) has at one time or another treated the homeless.

I see many more street people than I would have thought I'd see from the steps of the Capitol, and there's not one amongst us who shouldn't be saying "There but for the grace of God go I." Yes, you too, Senators.

I've twice spoken with a girl here who has spent her fair share of time on the streets, and she told me that straight up, the reason many of the people she knows are homeless is that they spend their disability checks on drinking and drugs instead of lodging.

The scoop from the "inside."

I also spoke to another man who's been homeless twice, and he told me it was his own fault, he made a lot of bad choices that landed him where he was. It was hard for him to come back, but now he's a business owner and has a family that he loves dearly.

For me, it's easier and more rewarding to help dogs. They rarely bite the hand that feeds them (ok, there was that one dog that tried to kill me, but still.)

I formerly volunteered at a woman's shelter, where they told me that on average most women go back to their abusive spouses seven times, and we weren't to say anything negative to them about it. That wasn't easy. Letting them step into the arms of abuse and saying "Good luck with that?"

I used to want to be a Natural Doctor, hence the B.S. and M.S. in Naturology, but I learned very quickly that humans don't listen well to advice and typically don't make the changes that they could/should make to live a better life. It was disheartening.

I'm no different, how often do I listen to advice, even if it's good? Rarely. I think we humans 'bite the hand that feeds us' much more quickly and more often than dogs do.

Regardless of whether humans are doing it to themselves are not, that's no excuse for us as a society not to have a safe place for all to sleep at night. We are absolutely failing by not doing so.

What did irritate me about the flyer this man passed out, was that **it claimed that America has lost our minds in part because we are worried about animal issues such as chaining,** implying that we put them before homelessness.

Really? Why does it have to be an either/or situation? Can't we address multiple social issues at a time? Surely we can treat our homeless with compassion and house and clothe them, and yet also advocate for better laws for our best friends?

There is plenty of goodwill available in the universe for every social issue to partake of. We don't need to belittle other issues in order to make a point about our own.

I believe that chained dogs deserve a hell of a lot better than they are getting. **Not a one of them ever asked to be chained for life, not a one of them committed a crime, and not a one of them is any different than the dog laying on your couch right now.**

I believe it is within the means of our senate and house to pass this bill before the session is over, despite what they say.

I heard that the Ag committee met today, and when they were asked if they discussed the tethering issue, the answer was no. *Really? Can you really be that callous toward the desires of your constituents, much less the needs of the dogs who are suffering and the children who are dying? Really?*

I believe they are choosing not to address our bill despite the overwhelming evidence that people want it.

I believe in miracles. I believe there are those with enough power to make things change for chained dogs.

That someone may just well be us. Don't let them off the hook. These dogs very lives depend on it.

I started creating 'art' every day with Magnum's poster and chain

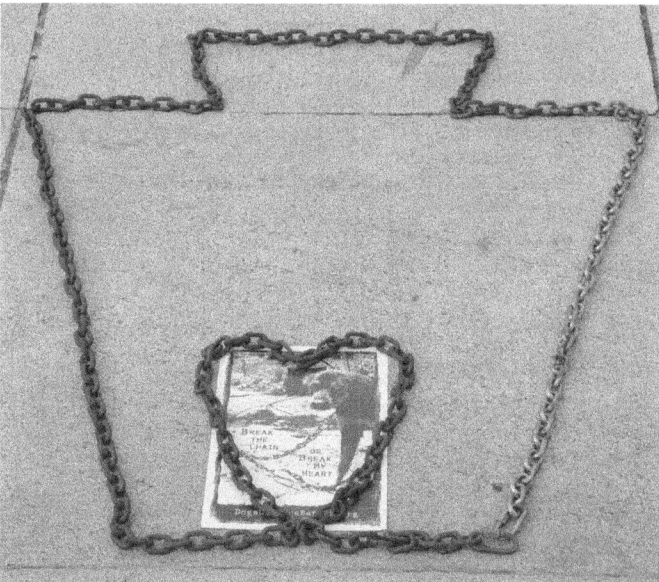

Day 37
Throw Us a Bone

September 21

☙❧

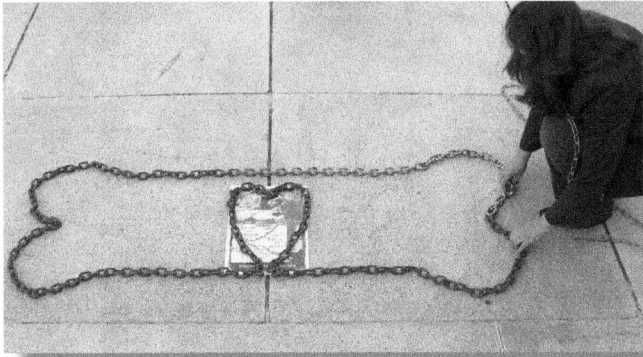

Creating the day's Magnum Art, a dog bone, of course!

I was feeling really down this morning. One of those "Why do I bother, I should have just stayed in bed" kinda' days, only with a chain and a doghouse on the Capitol steps rather than a desk at the office where you hate your boss.

Really, do you ever wonder why you bother? *I've sat here miserably for 37 days for these dogs, and they don't even discuss the bill in committee? Really?*

I sat on the steps and cried, for the third time—which I guess isn't too bad for 37 days on a chain—but then the universe threw me a bone, so to speak.

Senator Alloway, prime co-sponsor of SB1435, came out to talk to me, and he was a very nice guy. He sits next to Brubaker in caucus, and said that he's been trying to discuss it with him. He is absolutely willing to reintroduce at the beginning of next session.

Then a few other people introduced themselves, and I spoke to one rep, Thomas Murt, who was very caring and said he totally didn't understand what the hold-up was. It seemed like a no-brainer to him. He assured me he would support the bill when he got the chance.

I know the universe sent him to cheer me up because he said **"Don't be discouraged. This is how change is made, in ways like you're doing, so keep going."**

See, there are some good people, even in positions of power. We must cling to that.

The gas drilling rally that was supposed to take place on the steps beside me was inexplicably moved indoors at the last moment, really bumming me out…I was counting on that to entertain me for one hour out of the day!

The disappointment I felt when the rally moved inside reminded me of how a chained dog most feel when it rains on the family picnic in the yard.

For a brief period of time, the dog is not alone, he's provided with some visual stimulation, he's almost part of the family as they are playing and eating all around him. Maybe he's even thrown a bone.

Then suddenly it starts to rain, and everyone picks up their food and runs inside the house. **He is left suddenly alone again, and he—head hanging—sadly moseys back over to lay in the meager shade of the doghouse, his momentary respite from the pain of his solitude a brief memory.**

Day 38
Senators in Training

September 22

☙❧

Both the chained dogs and those who love them are brokenhearted

There was a rally on the steps today with a horrendous turn-out; it made our rally look like Woodstock. There were literally only seven people watching, and I think they were probably all campaign managers or aides.

The speakers were political candidates for the Senate who had banded together for the rally from various districts. I won't say which party it was to save them the embarrassment, but I'm not sure it even matters in the end. It seems to be so much rhetoric and promises just to get elected and then…it's all the same.

What did strike me as disheartening was the fact that all of them but one ignored my existence. One guy did say Hi and that he agreed with me, but didn't identify himself as a candidate and didn't introduce himself. I only knew he was up for election when I saw him speak.

Now, I've never run for office, and don't have much tolerance for bullshit, so would be horrible at it, but it seems to me your job as a candidate is to feign interest in the issues and the people and go up and meet them. In short, sell yourself.

Also, if you're running for office, I would assume you are watching the news or reading the newspaper enough to know what I'm doing here.

Yet not one of them came up to meet me or sell themselves to me, and/or in any way make me believe for one second that if they get into office they would support a bill for chained dogs.

I know I say this a lot, but I just can't help myself, I'm incredulous: Really?

When the guy asked if there were any questions, I yelled up from my chain "What will you do for chained dogs?" He looked at me and waved.

They actually are quite good senators in training.

Newsflash to prospective candidates who were at the Capitol today, as well as those already in office: Real dog lovers don't chain their dogs, and REAL dog lovers vote.

So it might behoove you to start paying attention to this issue.

A review of the people who might be angry that you pass a chaining law is as follows:

1. **People who chain their dogs**. These people will claim to 'love' their dogs, and will have a myriad of excuses for WHY

their dog lives 24/7 on a chain; but wife beaters claim to 'love' their wives too, how's that workin' out for the wife? These people rarely vote, and the few who do will not number enough to get you kicked out of office.

2. **Dogfighters.** If you pass a law limiting chaining, you are messing with their convenience, and giving law enforcement one more tool to put them out of business. What a shame.

3. **Breeders.** Most don't use chains, but they don't like anyone messing with their "rights" to do whatever they please with their "property." So if they don't use chains anyway, why would you listen to their flimsy reasons why they should be allowed to?

Are these the people whose votes you care about? Or do you care about the votes of the true doglovers, who know dogs deserve better, and who come from all walks of life, both parties, and are probably supporting your campaigns anyway?

Someone who works at the Capitol sent me this message, and made my day: "Don't lose hope and stay strong. I work at the Capitol and walk by you every day. I can say this: if we had any "representatives" in this state who devoted themselves to Pennsylvania's problems as much as you are doing for canine freedom, this state would not be in the mess it is in today. For as long as I have worked at the Capitol—I have seen many protests, many public speakings, etc; but they never get their point across because they are only there for a matter of a few hours. You, on the other hand, are getting A LOT of attention all over...not just Harrisburg. **Because of your dedication to what you believe, I think you are making a lot of people think about the issue a little deeper.** I just wanted to let you know, although the reps who work at Harrisburg can be blind in their ways, not all Pennsylvanian's are."

Day 39
What is Crazy, Anyway?

September 23

∞

I'm turning into a biker chick. Where's my Harley?

Before I officially formed Dogs Deserve Better in 2002, I decided to take a stand for chained dogs. I created a sign, a "No Chains" kind of thing with a picture of a dog in it, and I hung it in the window of my van. I felt scared about doing it, and as far as I knew at the time I was the only one taking such a stand, at least in my area.

My brother looked at the sign and said, *"I agree with you, but I would never put that in my window."*

I told my neighbor I was going to start an organization against chaining, and she said, *"I agree with you, but you'll never get any-where with that; no one will ever listen to you."* (Maybe she knows the legislators...)

I started the organization anyway, and guess what I've heard a thousand times in the past eight years, mostly from those who chain their dogs and leave ranting, screaming messages on my machine? "You're crazy."

They think if they just explain to me how Gosh Darn HAPPY their dog is on the chain, I'll finally understand and stop all this nonsense about dogs wanting to be with people.

Now THAT's crazy!

People who are passionate about social change which gives members of society rights that go against the ingrained hierarchy are often labeled as crazy.

Alice Paul, credited with finally winning women the right to vote, was thrown in jail with her followers for demonstrating in front of the White House everyday and embarrassing the President. They then attempted to have her committed as "crazy;" which would have been a very convenient end to their problem. Luckily they didn't succeed.

I've been called crazy repeatedly for standing in front of the Pennsylvania Capitol Building chained to a doghouse, mostly by those who are arguably unhappy in their own lives and are un-able to see the determination it takes to sacrifice so much for those in need.

The unhappy guy near me who sees only things like "I kiss my boyfriend and get off the chain for potty breaks" is a prime ex-ample of this mentality. I spend ten hours a day here for chained dogs, and that's what he takes away from it? I feel sorry for him. He is one miserable bastard.

And, guess what, nasty guy? I STILL kiss my boyfriend and get off my chain for potty breaks (for which you should be grateful.) Natty Natty Boo Boo.

There's one girl that I may need to put in my crazy compartment after today. She's a cute girl, thin, has dreads that she wears up in a black rasta hat, and she always dresses nice. She doesn't look crazy. She is usually seen walking two dogs on the other side of the street, but not seeming to notice what I'm doing or caring one way or the other about it.

One day early on she came over and sat down, asking me what I was doing. I explained, then I told her I liked her dogs. Her response? "They're not my dogs."

No "I'm a dog walker" or "They're my boyfriend's." Nothing. I was like, "Oh, OK."

She said nothing else for awhile, then got up and walked off.

She's continued to walk the same two "not her" dogs past me, and I've tried waving or smiling at her numerous times. She just looks the other way.

One day she was riding a bike past, and she put her hand up to shield her eyes so she didn't see me. Odd.

That's when I really started to wonder what the deal was with this girl.

This morning, though, she walked the two "not her" dogs on my side of the street, and half smiled at me as she walked by.

I thought "hmm, maybe she does like what I'm doing after all," but then she started crossing the street, stopped in the middle of the street, pulled her headphones off, and yelled "There will be less vet bills, do you really think they'll support that?"

WTF?

What is she talking about?

Joe and I just looked at each other, puzzled.

There will be less vet bills if we pass a law limiting chaining?

Pretty sure it's the opposite. For one thing, chained dogs are rarely vetted in any way, rarely have licenses, and rarely have even a rabies shot. Their caretakers are giving very few dollars to any vet.

If they give up the dog to rescue it results in MORE vet bills, not less, as we immediately get them vetted, spayed/neutered, and licensed.

Then, their adoptive homes and families—head and shoulders above the previous ones—will take the dogs to the vet faithfully all the years of the dogs' lives until they pass.

Therefore, rescuing a chained dog increases vet revenue. Mandating better care of dogs increases vet revenue (the vets really should be behind this law). DDB alone spent over $65,000 vetting formerly chained and penned dogs in our last fiscal year. The amount spent at vets if they were still on the chain? Negligible.

I'm still giving her the benefit of the doubt though, perhaps she could be autistic or have asperger's or something, and just think differently than I do?

Another guy, a tall, possibly homeless man with a speech impediment came up to me carrying a magazine and pages of writing. I think he was trying to explain to me how the two articles in the magazine were related, and he had gone to the library and taken all these notes, but none of it made sense to me. I felt bad for him, because he obviously had intelligence within him, but for whatever reason his logic was not understandable by others. It seemed, though, to make sense to him.

After that, a woman shook her head at my sign and mumbled "Why don't you attack the real problem." Normally when someone's mumbling and walking away, I just ignore them because they obviously don't want to engage about it. But I'd had enough for one day, so I loudly said "What is the real problem?"

She said "People who chain their dogs."

Oh. Duh! Why didn't I think of that?

I said "How do you stop them from chaining their dogs without a law that tells them they can't chain their dogs?"

I think we might really want to take a good look at the word 'crazy' before we go labeling the woman chained to the doghouse. Just sayin'.

Miscellaneous stuff from the day:

1. I started feeling sick in the afternoon, but I didn't know if it was from the heat or I picked up a virus that's been going around. I'm not keen on puking while chained.

2. A bug flew onto my shirt, Deb says they're stinkbugs. I thought I brushed it off of me, but turned out it went down into my shirt! I looked down and saw it crawling out from inside, and I squealed and flicked it off. I was totally freaked out.

3. I got off my chain today for the only thing besides a bathroom break that would make me do so: to help an animal. There was a kitten trapped in the engine of a car near the juice shop yesterday, and Steve, the juice guy, probably saved it's life because he put a note on the woman's car to check her engine before leaving. The kitten is feral, and it scratched her and ran away when she tried to get it out.

Then one of the guys who works at the Capitol came down and asked me if I help animals other than dogs. He told me there was a kitten crying up at the one window of the Capitol. So I went up, and sure enough it was the same kitten. I tried to get it, but we ended up in epic kitten fail...who knows where the poor thing is now.

Day 40
A Trip to Montana and Two Guest Blogs

September 24

Deb Smith, making some noise for chained dogs!

Wow, 40 Days! Who would have imagined it? My favorite line of the day, which I used on an interview with Channel 21 was "I've been wandering in the desert of Pennsylvania politics for 40 days now." Well, I thought it was funny.

I was speaking at a conference in Montana, and I couldn't let them and their chained dogs down, so I reluctantly (fine, it was jubilantly!) left at 1:00 to get to the airport for the flight to Montana. **I was so excited to be FREE!**

Deb Smith was the first to sit in for me. She wrote: Got there at 1:00 p.m. and Tami left. Five minutes later a car drove past and a guy yelled "F@*K YOU" at me. It makes me sad that there are such compassion-less people out there.

Then, I imagined myself as a chained dog. The only stimulation I got was when cars passed by and responded to my "HONK TO FREE CHAINED DOGS" sign. It was incredibly hot and boring, and I kept scouting the sun in the sky wondering how long it would be until I got some shade (was there until 3:45 and it never happened - just like it doesn't happen for chained dogs).

At one point, I heard a little thud on my sign; I looked at it and it was a STINK BUG, and I was actually happy to have some inquisitive company, LOL! GIMME SOME/ANY ATTENTION, with my tail wagging!

A nice lady named Sally stopped by. She was expecting to see Tami again, but was still kind enough to hold the sign and let me run over to the Smoothie Shop for a moment.

Gotta TRULY admit—I could never do what Tami has been doing day in and day out—I was so pleased to see my replacement chainees, Cherie and Justin, who finished out the day in Tami's absence. And that was only 2.5 hours!

***

Wedding Party and a Trolley
by Cherie Smith and Justin Strawser

We sat in for Tami Friday afternoon for 2.5 hours. It was a hot day (even though autumn has officially arrived). We came prepared though with water but it wasn't too long until the shade brought us relief. Justin wanted to chain himself for the entire time we were there and complained often of boredom.

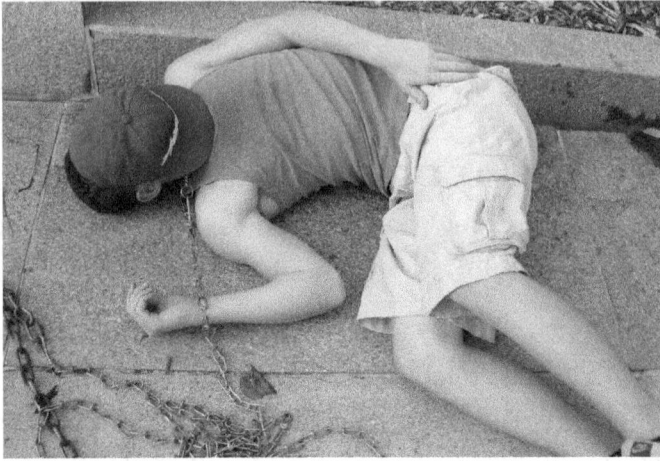

Around 4:30, people started to arrive at the Capitol all dressed up (mostly in black). The women who arrived were beautiful and reminded me of the Emmy's and the red carpet—I felt under-dressed in my shorts and t-shirt.

As they walked past, I noticed their high heels, short dresses, tan bodies, and each person who arrived completely ignored us except for a younger woman in her late teens or early twenties. She was holding her boyfriend's hand and looked down at the dog house and said, "Awe, what a cute puppy" in a high pitched voice and then walked away.

Justin turned to me and said, "How can she say what a cute puppy when this dog is clearly chained?" My response, "It just shows the ignorance of people and is why we are here—to educate."

Tami may not see herself as strong but anybody who has the guts and determination to sit at the Capitol for 10 hours a day in the heat, rain, thunder, and lightening deserves respect. Thank you Tami for giving up your freedom to help free all of the dogs who wait day in and day out. It's not right.

Day 41
Short but Not So Sweet

September 27

☙❧

Ginger Cayo and Deb Warner stand in an all day rain

Guest chainees Ginger Cayo and Deb Warner from State College, PA, kept their blog entry short but not so sweet: "We were both soaking wet. The only dry spot was about six inches of our jeans on the front of our thighs. I can't imagine how Tami has done this for 41 days! At least we had each other to talk to. Having experienced this ourselves now, we're totally in awe. To be chained all day . . . think of the very intelligent breeds like the German Shepherd; no wonder they go crazy! Nowhere to go but the end of a chain, nothing to do day after day.

Day 42
Another Day in the Rain for Fellow Chainees

September 28

๑๑

Kel Hatt, lucky enough to draw another day in the rain.

Apparently there were four guest chainees on Tuesday, and I only have blog entries from two of them, but you'll get the hint that it was another rainy day in Central PA.

From Kel Hatt: During my post of guarding the dog house, a man walked up and explained he's a college professor at West Chester University. He said he agrees with the dog legislation we're trying to get passed and asked if he could video tape the scene for his class to use as an example of citizens getting involved. He videoed for about 3-4 minutes up close of the dog house, chain, myself, everything. Then he recorded a few questions he asked me along with my answers. Basically what I was hoping to accomplish by being there; I hope it brings more attention to the topic. I figured heck...the more people who see his video the better. Let's get the word out, everyone!

From Betty Harris: I've been here an hour and was fortunate enough to talk to several people. Most were very interested in our cause and wanted to know how they could help. Even though the temperature was in the 70's and there was a breeze, the sun was hot. I can't imagine how a dog, wearing a fur coat, must feel, especially with the very hot, humid days we had this summer.

This chain is heavy on my neck, and I am very bored. I've been lucky that people have stopped to chat. I know how bored dogs are in the shelter even with the interaction staff and volunteers give them. I can't imagine how boring a chained dog's life must be.

People are interesting. Most avoid looking directly at you. I imagine I've done the same in the past. I will definitely think about acting differently under similar circumstances in the future.

God bless your work, Tami.

Anna Giza created Love Me chain art, and wrote:
For the "unloved." You ARE LOVED by US . . . never forgotten by US. . .

Barb Shaffer spent time on the chain in my stead as well.

Day 43
Don't Drag Me Back to That Chain!

September 29

Must Love Dogs.

I was off my chain for 4-1/2 days; it proved to be about 2-1/2 too many, because in that time I went soft—I wanted nothing to do with going back on that chain, no matter how I tried to convince myself that I had to.

I've seen chained dog caretakers dragging their dogs back to the chain when they escape or are left off for a rare bout of freedom, and NOW I truly know that feeling. I wanted to throw a royal fit, throw myself on the ground, and kick and scream.

I am astounded by the dedication fellow Pennsylvania dog

lovers showed in my absence...I had thought I would have to leave the spot vacant while I was gone—at a crucial time during a four day session for the Senate—but no, Mike Romberger arranged volunteer chainees for all day Tuesday, and arranged to pick up the dog house each day and deliver it the next morning.

How can I even adequately describe the beauty of Montana? How surreal was it to leave a chain Friday afternoon, and Saturday morning wake up to mountains of grandeur surrounding my hotel room?

Sure, I found chained dogs there, just like here, and sure they need to tackle the problem too, but my eyes were so glued to the supreme FREEDOM represented by the mountains, woods, and miles and miles of uninhabited landscapes that I could believe it a utopia if such a thing existed.

I felt at peace there, and that's saying a lot with the chaos of my life. I told Joe I wanted to move there, but he reminded me that was probably only in the summer. OK, he's probably right.

We drove from Spokane, Washington, up to Canada, took a two-hour jaunt through Canada, and back down into the U.S., at which time we were pulled over and searched—they were sure we must be drug dealers meeting our contact across the border or something. They are probably less suspicious when you stay for a week or so, but we were naively sightseeing and didn't think anything about it.

On Monday I found out my son Rayne had the flu, and I wasn't there for him. He seems to get sick a lot when I travel, and will give him another reason to hate me when he's older, I presume. He stayed home from school on Tuesday, but made it back to school today, so only missed one day.

As if I didn't feel guilty enough about that, while I was here chained this morning, I got a call from my assistant that two of the foster dogs had gotten into a fight, and she had a very hard time breaking it up. She was crying, and once again, the guilt piled onto my head that I'm not there for my other obligations while I sit here on this chain fighting a losing battle with people who really intend to take no action on our bill despite my efforts, your efforts, and what the people want.

I was really THIS close (picture my thumb and forefinger only a fraction of an inch apart) from walking away from this today. This close. Only stubbornness kept me here, sheer stubbornness.

I believe now that we've lost this fight, and the dogs will spend another winter freezing to death and being disposed of by criminals who won't get caught. Children will be attacked, seriously injured, and die before we try again to pass a law protecting them from the effects of chaining.

To make matters worse, tomorrow has 100% chance of rain, heavy rain, and there's a flood warning in effect. I guess we know what my day looks like. I can't help but wonder if I will make it through. With my resolve cracking and fracturing and guilt about my home life and work piling onto my head, will I be able to withstand the four inches of rain we are forecast to get?

When I feel there's no point to it?

Senator Brubaker walked by on the other side of the stairs this afternoon, pretending he didn't see me of course, but I know he did. I know he looked at me.

Mike, when it's pouring down rain tomorrow, I'll be sitting in the exact same spot you saw me in today. I hope I have the courage to stay there all day for chained dogs.

Miscellaneous stuff from today:

1. I only got 3.5 hours sleep last night, because I didn't get in from Montana until midnight. It was a very, very long day, and I kept falling asleep propped up onto my elbow.

2. There is a dinosaur exhibit inside the Capitol. Someone said it was a real one, and maybe it was, I'm no expert, but you'd think they wouldn't drag the real thing around like that. I took a quick look on a potty break. It had a really little head.

There were many parents with kids coming to look at it today, and lots and lots of them stopped to explain to their kids what I was doing outside, which was nice. Inevitably, I ran into at least one chainer who argued with me about what he should do with his dog if we pass a law...Um, bring it in the house? Build it a fence? Meet its needs? He's also the one who let his bratty little daughter destroy my Magnum Chain Art of the day without saying a word to her. What a nice gentleman.

3. Some findings from the studies Mike gave me:

A. Studies of "backyard dogs" (these were dogs not chained but not allowed inside with the people) have shown:

They spend most of their time traveling between one door of the house and another door, window, or gate. Why? To be with the humans!

Dogs spent the majority of their inactive time near the house, particularly near the door or gate. Why? They want to be with US!

*From Amanda Jane Kobelt et al., Australia

B. Studies of "shelter dogs" and what they show preference for found:

Dogs in the study showed greater preference for contact with humans compared to dogs or toys. Second only to food. Contact with humans was considered not a luxury but a "necessity."

*From ISAH 2005 - Warsaw

C. Studies of "test dogs" and what they show preference for found:

"It is especially intriguing that the presence of the human caretaker significantly reduced the glucocorticoid [stress] response of dogs."

[When the caretaker is present] the dog clearly paid great attention to the caretaker.

Indicates the importance of human contact.

*From Behavior and Glucocorticoid Responses
of Adult Domestic Dogs, Tuber et. Al. 1996

A handwritten card from supporters and friends.

Day 44
Chained in the Rain: for the Dogs

September 30

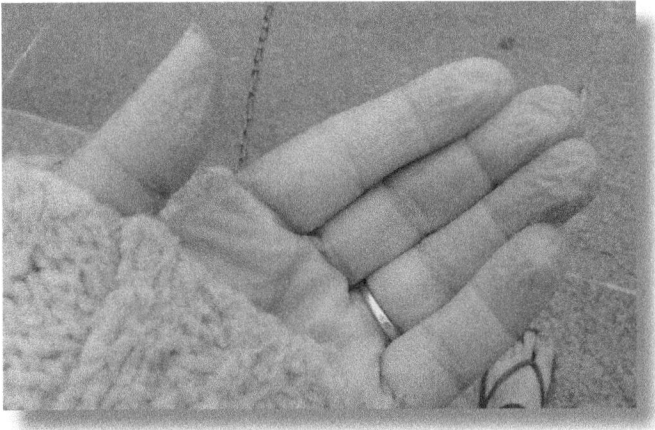

My hands after seven hours in the rain.

Day 44 found me chained in the rain for much of the day, no umbrella, no rain gear...what else do I have to give them? I have spent 44 days chained to a doghouse at the PA State Capitol, and they are still ignoring both my (our) activities and the plight of these dogs.

There's no word big enough to describe the anguish that fact brings me.

You can watch the video log of the day at this YouTube link: http://youtu.be/I0H3xIO5yT0.

Days 45-46
Where Liberty Dwells There is My Country

October 4

☙❧

Note the phrase "Where Liberty Dwells There is My Country" behind me.

This blog really isn't about liberty. It's about the opposite of liberty, but my favorite picture captured by Joe contains the words "Where Liberty Dwells..." and I'm beside it, a little blurry, standing on a chain in the rain.

Do you ever wonder why people say hurtful things and never seem to notice that they are saying hurtful things and just go blithely along like they're your long lost best friend or something?

Of course, I rarely call them on it. I just take it and then wonder later why I didn't, ever so politely, say "And you felt a need to tell me that why? Do you realize I'm undergoing a day of pure hell here and you really feel a need to come out and tell me that Heidi Prescott told you that the House reps and senators laugh at me in there?"

First things first, though: **yesterday was truly the worst day of my chaining EVER, hands down.** (Have I said that before? Well, they can come along and top each other...)

I debated with myself about whether it really topped the day of 105 degree heat index. There's a chance that in the midst of that day, I would have felt that a day of 48 degrees and solid rain was a walk in the park, but it's the next morning and I still think yesterday was worse.

Every bone in my body and every muscle still hurts after 12 hours. My butt was so cold I thought it had fallen off, but alas, it's still back there boppin' around.

Of course, time does blur the true horribility of any day. Yes, I said horribility. I don't care if it's a real word, it fits and I'm using it.

The best thing about yesterday is that I didn't engage in a pity party. I don't think I could have made it through if I'd have spent time poor me-ing. I really don't know how I made it through. Sheer determination.

I paced 10 steps out and 10 steps back on my chain for at least 7.5 hours of the day. I did it because if I stopped and sat down, not only did I get wetter, but I got colder as well, and it was just too unbearable to be any colder and wetter than I already was. So I had no choice but to pace or leave. Leaving wasn't an option, so I paced.

Countless times, even though I knew it was 10 steps out, I jerked at the end of my chain in surprise because I was nearly catatonic and was just walking like I could go forever.

But I couldn't.

That's called lack of liberty.

In some odd way, the day actually went quicker than you would imagine it could. I think because I was in a state where I was a walking, pacing zombie. My phone was in the doghouse, so I didn't know what time of the day it was, and I just existed.

Just existed; cold, wet, and on a chain.

Like a dog.

Which reminds me, back to the senators and reps. Of course they're laughing at me in there. That's what bullies do when they are confronted with someone with more courage than they have in their little finger. Someone who has the nerve to stand up and say "Wait a second, this just isn't right."

They ridicule them and taunt them and bully them until they die of abuse or grow a bigger backbone than these guys will ever have in their wildest dreams.

I guess it will remain to be seen which happens to me.

There are one or two reps in there, though, that I truly admire. I'm not going to say their names here because the bully reps will probably just go and laugh at them and pick on them and call them names for being kind to a woman who dares to take a stand in their front yard.

[OK, fine, it was Scavello and Murt. The cat's out of the bag.]

You know when you bully in school these days you get your ass suspended. Just sayin'.

These two reps that I'm thinking of are both House reps, and they both NEVER fail to treat me with respect. They speak to me, and they ask me how I am, and if I need anything. The one is new, and not jaded yet, but I feel in my gut that he's a genuinely nice man. I thank him for his kindness.

It's sad that you want to cry when someone shows you kindness, because it's the exception rather than the rule.

It's sad that you have to focus on NOT crying most of the day, when you're standing in the rain and people still walk by you like you don't even exist.

It's sad that our world is full of people who don't even care that people die on the street and children die by chained dog attacks and dogs freeze to death on the end of the chain.

And Pennsylvania is still the only state in the country with enough bullies that we think it's ok to dump pigeons out of a box and blast them away for target practice. You're bullies with guns. Pick on someone your own size.

At least I'm closer to your size than those poor pigeons. You sicken me.

I went and bought Nelson Mandela's autobiography last night for inspiration. I can't imagine what he went through…I need to see how he made it out to the other side, how he possibly continued to believe that change was possible even in the midst of years of prison. What was the key to his success?

I need such a key.

I'm compiling a Top Ten list of annoying things people say to me while I'm chained. Yes, "They laugh at you in there" will be making the list, maybe even number 1, but also "They aren't going to do anything with your bill" is right up there.

Please stop feeling the need to come out and tell me that. I know it firsthand.

Thank you.

Day 47
Top Ten Most Annoying Things People Say to Me While I'm On This Chain

October 5

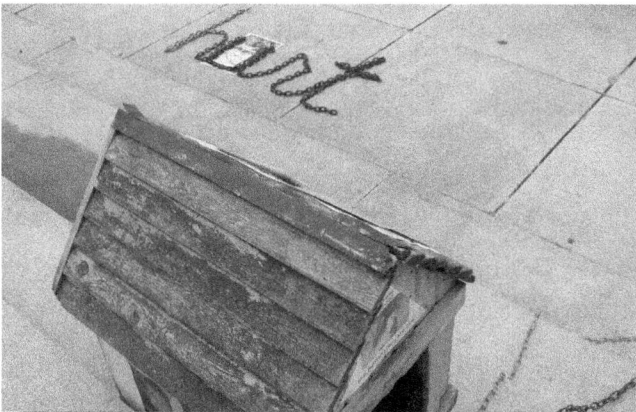

Chains hurt both dogs and people

As promised, my top ten list of things people say to me while I'm chained out here that frankly, annoy the crap outta me…and most of them happen over and over again.

10. Oh, I don't chain MY dog.

Good! Now realize maybe you should help OTHER dogs that look just like yours and are living chained. Freedom is about ALL of us, not just some.

9. What if the dog likes being on a chain?
What? Yeah, me, me, put ME on this chain! Ooh, Ooh, pick ME!

8. Aren't you taking this to extremes?
Well, since I don't have my law, apparently it hasn't yet been taken to the extremes to which it needs to be taken.

7. If I take my dog off a chain, and he bites someone, who's responsible for that?
You, dumbshit. We aren't saying take them off and let them run the neighborhood. We're saying take them in the house, build them a fence and a doggie door, walk them on a leash. You know, be RESPONSIBLE for their welfare and safety.

6. Is there a dog in there? (looking into my doghouse.)
OK, I can stomach this one from children…because, well, they're children. But you adults? Come on, get with the program.

5. What will people do with their dogs if you get this law and they work at night and have to chain their dog while they're at work?
Um, get responsible, same as the people who work during the day? I know this for a fact, and it was confirmed by both the humane officer and the animal control officer we took with us to meet with Brubaker's assistant, that there are VERY few dogs chained while people go to work. Why? Because they're responsible! Their dog lives in the home with them, and they find a better way to keep him/her while they're working. Most

people use chaining in two ways: 24/7 constant chaining, and 15 minute tethering potty breaks. Very few people are in between those two extremes.

4. You know your bill isn't going anywhere this session.

Good Lord…I know I'm on a chain, but do I look like I'm crawling out from under a ROCK? I've been told personally twice by Brubaker's personal assistant that they have a problem with the time limit…as in the fact that there IS one. Oh, yes, and your bill isn't going anywhere this session because the Republican Caucus doesn't want it to. That doesn't make it right or doesn't make me walk away.

3. So and So told me they laugh at you in there.

And we laugh at them out here. Now, let's all put on our big girl and boy pants and get a law passed. Oh, and what is that Gandhi quote? *"First they ignore you, then they ridicule you, then they fight you, then you win."* Damn, I was pretty much hoping we were at the winning stage…but we seem to have slipped back to ridiculing and ignoring.

2. [Snicker snicker. Whisper whisper. Glance glance. Repeat.]

Granted, they aren't really talking TO me…but about me, and I can see them doing it. Geez, just come up and ask me, that's what I'm here for! I'm not one to yell out to strangers, but I'm more than happy to talk to anyone who is interested.

1. [I don't see you. You are invisible. Now go away and stop embarrassing yourself…oh, and me, of course.]

OK, they're not really talking to me here, either. This is all signaled to me through alien antenna and body language…but I get the general drift. So sorry to embarrass you!

Oh, no, actually I'm not. Now go away, you've made my #1 of the annoying list, and I just don't want to see your smug "I'm better than you, because you're obviously a homeless person or in league with them" face anymore.

OK, now I feel oh, so much better now! Let's find a chained dog picture to remind me that I'm here for them, and not the humans who continue to foil both me and them.

This little dog has been on a chain in my middle school boyfriend's yard for at least the past eight years. I've tried everything to get the dog a better life, and he has repeatedly ignored me. Well, he was a horrible kisser anyway. The boyfriend, not the dog. I'm sure the dog gives great puppy smooches.

Day 48
My Top Ten Gratitude List

October 6

⊗⊗

Cold and rain don't mix, and I endured a lot of it at the end

Although the Top Ten Pet Peeves may be more fun, I feel a need to balance it out with the Top Ten things I'm grateful for from living chained at the PA State Capitol for 48 days. This may be more difficult…but here goes.

10. (Damn, I'm stuck already…) OK, I'm going to say **the two reps who are kind to me. [Scavello and Murt.]** I know there must be a few more that are actually kind, caring human beings. Right? I just haven't met most of them yet.

9. **Weight loss.** Granted, it was no spa treatment, and I probably only lost ten pounds before Joe kindly found me gluten free snacks which helped me gain back five of them (thank you, baby—I know, it's my choice to eat them.) But any weight loss is good weight loss, so I hereby proclaim myself grateful for it.

8. The **Juicy Rumors juice bar**, because this is where I got my daily FRESH juice and used the bathroom. Sadly, Steve has decided to go out of business, so now I have no more juice and have to schlep into the Capitol and through the metal detector to use the bathroom. But I AM grateful for the weeks and weeks I had juice and a closer bathroom.

7. **Lorena Marques and her crew** who came from New York and filmed for their project…and then stopped back by PA to take one of our rescues to New York to foster and find a home for him there. Turns out Stitch is a natural New York City dog, is adopted and doing great. And **Daly Agostino** who filmed for her project and stayed to take great footage of me being poured upon in the first deluge.

6. The many **regulars who just walk by and say Hi to me every morning**. They cheer me up by acknowledging my existence. There's the McDonald's worker who always looks so depressed…but now that I give him a big smile every morning, he actually seems cheerier when he walks by. There's the two laborers who always pass by, the guy of oriental descent walking quickly ahead, and the guy of Hispanic descent always lagging behind. The front guy gives me a cheery good morning, and now even the second guy smiles and says good morning. I think me acknowledging his existence cheers him up too!

Then there's the former Marine who is astounded that I even stand in the rain without an umbrella. On Monday he saluted me in the rain, and told me "You are tougher than a Marine drill sergeant." Now that's high praise indeed!

There's also the lawyer across the street who I've never actually spoken to, but he brings his golden retriever to work with him every morning, and gives me a wave along the way.

5. **The awareness we've raised for chained dogs.** People say "Too bad you didn't get media" but we actually got quite a bit of media which you can see linked from the site at fidos-freedom.com…many, many people now know more about this issue and want it to end. The city of Harrisburg passed a resolution urging the Senate to vote yes to anti-tethering. And many, many people wrote to Brubaker and the committee members, as well as their own senators and House reps. We may think they fell on deaf ears, but you can never be sure about that… we're building a wall of education, and sooner or later their wall of ignorance will collapse and we will come out as the winners we deserve to be!

4. **My room at the Radisson.** I received an amazing discount thanks to wonderful contacts through CPAA and a staff that really cares about animals…and with donors who stepped up to help cover the cost, it became manageable and the universe provided!

3. **The strength I've gained as a result.** Everyone says "I couldn't do that." I think all of us could do that (or anything) if it were that important to us. Never underestimate yourself and your abilities! Seeing Kim Jayne sitting in the rain ALL NIGHT LONG in Chicago's Chain Off in 2008 really inspired me, and every time I sit in the rain I think of her. **No one even knows she did it, there are no pictures of her doing it, but it's burned into my brain, and I wish I could put it into a picture so the world could see how dedicated she was for chained dogs.** Thank you for inspiring me, Kim.

2. **All the friends I've made through doing this** or who have stepped up to be part of my support team. Mike and Stacey Romberger, who have been integral from the first week, Melissa Swauger who visits me every day she can, Cathie MacArthur who I just met and who has become a faithful and dear friend, Barb Hacker, Deb Carr, Gordon Bakalar, Darryl Ragantesi, Mark and Barb Shaffer, Deb Smith, Cherie Smith and Justin Strawser, Deb Warner, Ginger Cayo, Kel Hatt, Betty Harris, and Anna Giza, all who took turns on the chain while I was in Montana.

And **all of you who've supported from a distance**…offering constant and daily words of encouragement, and sending letters to help buoy me up. *Even if they got returned to you, I'm still grateful you sent them!*

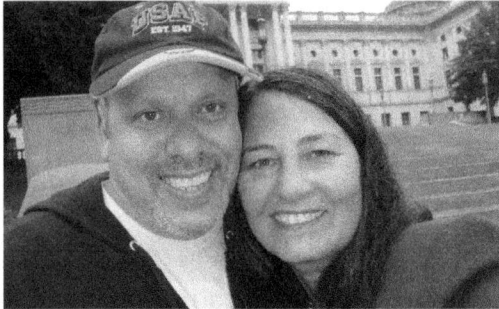

1. **And, always Joe, Rayne, and Brynnan.** This has been a very trying period for my family…they've missed me, they've done without me, and they've had to put up with very little of me or me at my very stressed. Joe has done his absolute best to help me each and every chance he's gotten…he comes up on his days off, he works on my house while I'm gone, he does all the heavy lifting when he's around, and brings me iced tea. **He has let me cry on his shoulder more than a few times since the beginning, and he has propped me up when I don't think I can do it another minute. He has been there for me, and I'm truly blessed and grateful for every moment of his presence in my life.**

Day 49
A Short Play on Pitbulls

October 7

☙❧

Pitbulls are chained more than any other breed

What follows is a short play that took place on the Capitol steps.

[Overweight, older white man with cane walks down steps behind woman chained to doghouse.]

Him: If it's a pitbull, you'd better just leave it on that chain.

Me: What? [Pretending I don't hear.]

Him: If it's a pitbull, leave it there.

Me: The pitbull should be in the house, then you don't have to worry about the chain at all.

Him: You can't have a pitbull in the house.

Me: Pitbulls are just like every other dog, and want to be with people more than anything else.

Him: Bah.

[Walks away.]

This one-act play on the steps of the Capitol today was brought to you by the chained lady and the overweight guy with the baseball cap. [Curtsy, bow.]

How can people be so grossly misinformed?

Now, I don't claim to be a pitbull expert, no more than I am a shepherd expert or an Akita expert. But I am a chained dog expert, and I can tell you this with 100% certainty: **Pitbulls are THE most-abused dogs in America, they are the most-chained dogs in America, and they are owned by some of the biggest idiots in America.**

Then we wonder why so many of them are involved in dog attacks? Look at the circle, people…here's what we do to the dog…and then here's what the dog does to us…

You give a pitbull to a thug, he's going to do one of three things with the dog: fight the dog, chain the dog (and then fight the dog or forget about the dog), or abuse the dog. Either way, that dog is going to turn mean just to save it's own skin.

I would too.

To review, the three biggest bite factors come from a male/unneutered/chained dog. If people stopped chaining all these pits, and socialized them with people from a young age, the fear-mongering would stop.

There are so many great groups working for pits out there…I highly commend you all! I know you have it tough, and we are in there with you getting pitties off chains as we can.

Educate yourself and others about pits and don't leave your kids alone with ANY dog. Dogs are strong, they can do a lot of damage if they want to, and often they don't respect children. It can be a very bad combination.

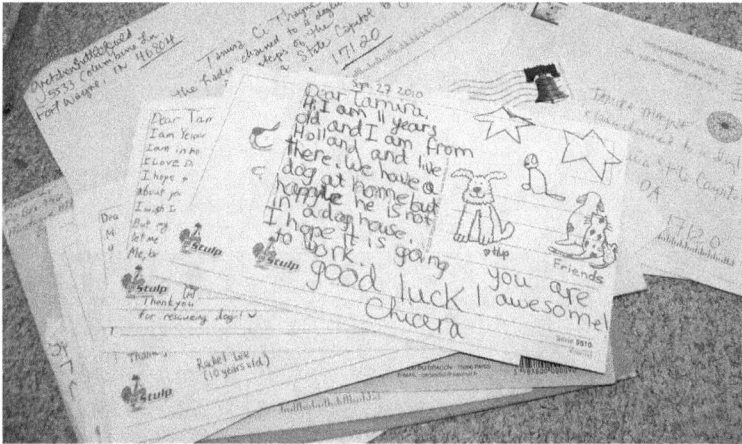

Miscellaneous stuff from today:

I got nine postcards from 10/11 year old students in the Netherlands. They said really cool stuff like:

"My name is Spencer and I'm 10. I heard about you from the yahoo homeschooler group. I really like what you're doing. One reason I am going to try to help your cause is because I love animals... Thank you for making me aware of this sad reality."

"I'm Hannah, am eleven years old, I come from Holland, and I saw your video on the internet and thought you're crazy, but no, it's super what you're doing so I hope the law changes."

"My name is Alona, and I'm from Israel. I love dogs and I even have one. I live in Holland and I'm 11 years old. Thank you for fighting for the dogs."

Day 50
She Escaped Her Chain!

October 8

☙❧

Deb Smith does it again, that girl's a trooper!

I escaped my chain today. And DAMN that felt good!

I know that the dogs don't typically get to do this…but every once in awhile, they break free and run amok, sometimes without good consequences. Let's pretend I was one of the ones who broke free and just get to enjoy their freedom for awhile before being slapped back on that chain.

In my case I got off my chain at noon to attend an Air Force reunion in Texas that I committed to prior to knowing how long my chaining would go on or even IF it would go on at all.

I was majorly excited about my weekend of freedom from not only the horrendous daily grind of living on this chain, but also the weekend grind of catching up on work I missed all through the week when I was chained.

I felt really and truly FREE for the first time in a long time! I treasured that feeling.

I was faced with shutting down early, but supporters Deb Smith and Ginger Cayo stepped up to cover my hours, and Deb took the house home with her to bring it back to me Monday. See, dogs, there ARE many other people out there who feel strongly about your freedom, and we are all working for you.

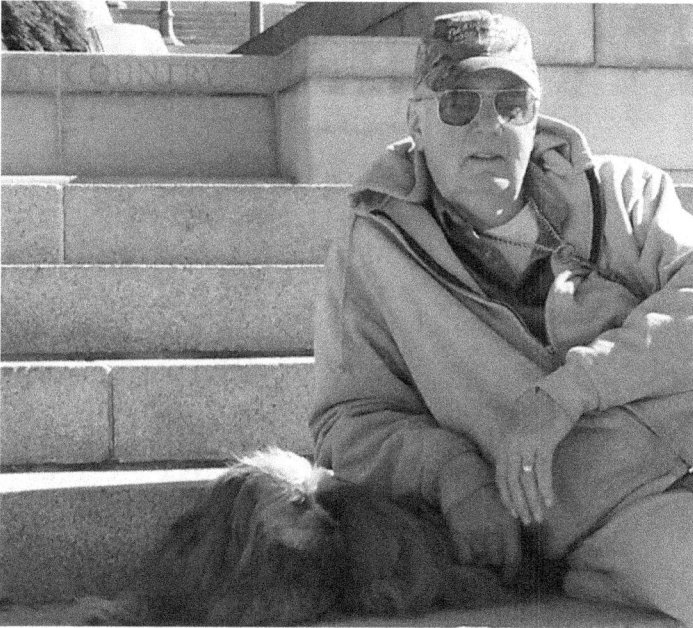

Gordon brought his cute little dog Cricket over; she looks like the dog on the cartoon version of the Grinch, so adorable!

Day 51
Those Crazy Holidays

October 11

Smiling and relaxed from my weekend of freedom, which the dogs never get...

I spent the weekend in Sugarland, Texas, at the 20th reunion of the Augsburger Air Force peeps. Of course, it's only my second time attending, since Facebook came along we all starting finding out about it and reconnecting...so that's a really cool thing.

Oddly enough, Joe and I had some major plane issues both on the way out and on the way back. The first time the plane behind us noticed our #2 engine smoking, and they found that to be a bit problematic. Of course I was annoyed, but who can argue with staying alive over losing two hours of talking about the olden days?

Then on the way home our plane had hydraulic problems, causing us to again switch planes and again lose two hours. Weird.

Needless to say, this also caused me to lose more sleep last night, and I was lucky that today was some holiday that only government workers get off—Columbus Day—so I could get away with doing a half day. No one was working at the Capitol anyway today; it was pretty much a ghost town.

I was even going to read my Nelson Mandela book for some inspiration while I was sitting there, but alas I must have left it either on the plane or in Joe's backpack.

Well, five hours of boredom beats ten hours of boredom any day of the week.

Thing is, I know it's winding down, I know we don't have hope left at this point, but I am determined to stick around until the session is over. I committed to it, and once committed, I need to see it through until it is indisputably without hope. And that would be the last day of the session.

I need to stay here just as long as those men and women who are ignoring our bill, to be in their faces every day, to be seen, and to put the idea into their heads that we'd better start taking this issue seriously.

So I HAVE to stick it out, have to stay here, even though I have a bad case of short-timer-itis.

For the dogs!

Day 52
Announcement: I Will Leave
The Capitol Steps Thursday, October 14

October 12

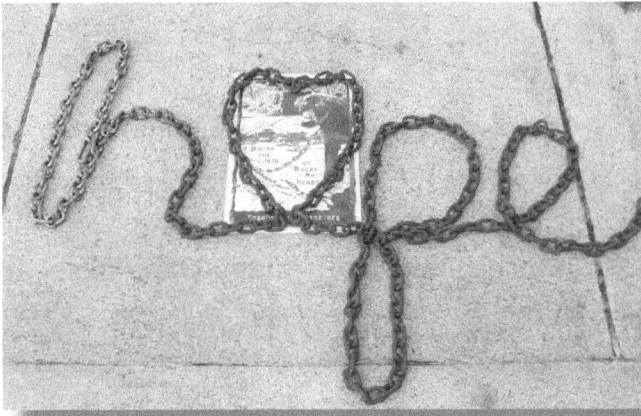

Hope, it's all we have left, and it's rapidly extinguishing

The Senate's last day of session is Thursday, October 14, 2010. What does this mean for our bill? That's its DEAD day. If we want to revive it, we have to start all over again next session, and work our way from the ground up. New bill number, new sponsors, new everything. So today I announced that Thursday will be my last day. The release follows:

WOMAN TO LEAVE CAPITOL STEPS
AFTER 52 DAYS CHAINED TO DOGHOUSE

WILL HOLD PRESS CONFERENCE FROM CHAIN BEFORE LEAVING

October 12, 2010 - Harrisburg, PA - Dog activist Tamira Ci Thayne, whose name roughly translates to "Peaceful Dog Warrior," will pack up her doghouse and return home to Blair County on Thursday.

Thayne will hold a press conference from her doghouse at the bottom of the Capitol steps on Thursday, October 14, at 11:00 a.m. at which time she will issue a statement about the bill and her 52 days on a chain.

The move is not without regret on her part. "As much as I hate to go home without a law for these dogs, the legislature's failure to pass a law protecting the children and dogs makes it necessary for us to begin anew in January. Meanwhile, dogs will die due to living chained in the harsh upcoming winter, and children will be attacked as a result of the aggressiveness bred by chaining."

During the short time Thayne was chained on the Capitol steps, three children in Pennsylvania made the papers from chained dog attacks. Little Alaha Crutchfield, 6, was described as being 'nearly scalped' by the dog who broke his chain to attack her.

Brianna Shanor, 8, died due to a chained dog attack in January 2009.

Thayne continues, "Dogs enhance our lives and protect us everyday, from assisting us as seeing eye and therapy dogs, to protecting the public at airports, protecting police officers, and protecting our troops at war. It is ridiculous that the state of Pennsylvania cannot provide some basic protections from the cruel practice of 24/7 tethering.

Continuous tethering is passive cruelty and neglect, and the time for this abuse has ended. While continuous tethering may not be as overtly obvious as someone beating a dog, it is equally as cruel and deprives a dog of what studies show is a necessity to him/her: human interaction and socialization. Pennsylvania must do something to protect the dogs and the children from the dangerous impacts of 24/7 chaining."

Thayne has spent each Monday through Friday, 8 a.m.-6 p.m., chained to her doghouse since August 2, 2010. During that time she abstained from eating and drank very little to simulate the life of a chained dog. She sweltered in the heat and endured all-day downpours without an umbrella. She lived as a chained dog, and she suffered as a chained dog.

She is the founder and CEO of Dogs Deserve Better, an organization dedicated to ending the chaining and penning of dogs and bringing them into the home and family. To read her daily blogs from the campaign, visit the site at www.fidosfreedom.com, or visit the organization's site at www.dogsdeservebetter.org.

Day 53
Who's Afraid of Failure?

October 13

☙❧

My doghouse might be smaller, but it has a bigger heart

I was always afraid of failure, since the time I was a young girl. I remember working at an ad agency in my mid-20's where the owners were a bumbling idiot and his wife who was overly fond of the bottle (maybe because of his idiot status.)

I couldn't imagine how they had the guts and courage and brains to start their own business and think that it would ever succeed.

Yet, there they were, moderately successful.

I came to the conclusion that they were just too stupid to fear failure, and extrapolated further that maybe all businesses were owned by stupid people because the smart ones were too busy figuring out all the ways they could fail to make a go of it.

That was a long time ago, and maybe I was a tad bit erroneous in that thinking. There are plenty of smart people who overcame their fears and started their own businesses or organizations. I even like to consider myself one of them.

I started my own freelance graphic designer business at home for a book publisher after my son was born almost 18 years ago. I have somehow managed to keep a roof over our heads ever since, although there were many months and many days I didn't know where the next dollar was coming from, or where the next client would come from.

Yet come they did, with a little faith.

When I started Dogs Deserve Better, I ran it the same way (the only way I knew how)—on a wing and a prayer. Somehow, eight years later, **we are still afloat and still advocating for chained dogs the world over.** I give credit for that in large part to great people who have come together to make a difference in this issue; employees, volunteers, and awesome area reps.

I have lost many battles—Doogie and this law come to mind as the biggest—and I'm not here to try to tell you it's enjoyable or I like it.

What I am here to tell you is that I'm still standing.

Mike Romberger used this Teddy Roosevelt quote in an article he wrote the other day on the Operation Fido's Freedom page, and I'd like us all to ponder it and remember it for future failures:

"It is not the critic who counts; not the man who points out how the strong man stumbles, or where the doer of deeds could have done them better. The credit belongs to the [wo]man who is actually in the arena, whose face is marred by dust and sweat and blood, who strives valiantly; who errs and comes short again and again; because there is not effort without error and shortcomings; but who does actually strive to do the deed; who knows the great enthusiasm, the great devotion, who spends [her]self in a worthy cause, who at the best knows in the end the triumph of high achievement and who at the worst, if [s]he fails, at least [s]he fails while daring greatly. So that [her] place shall never be with those cold and timid souls who know neither victory nor defeat."

I may feel like quitting right now, but I will rest for a week, I will mourn the loss of a helping hand for "my people," and I will get back up and fight again.

The chained dogs ARE my people. They are still not free. They ARE still suffering. Legislators HAVE failed them by their unwillingness to even consider a law which would aid these dogs and the children they in turn harm through fear and lack of socialization with humans.

I am not through here. This war is not over until we win. Fight with me.

Day 54
I Am Gone

October 14

☙❧

The dry spot where my doghouse used to be.

As fate would have it, Day 54 was a day of solid rain, from 9 a.m. throughout the entire day. I didn't know how I could make myself stay there for another tortuous day when it was pointless…but all the supporters reminded me of why I'm doing this…for the dogs, of course.

I wore two shirts, two sweaters, pantyhose, lined pants,

boots, gloves, and a winter coat, and I was still soaked to the bone and shivering.

The press conference was in the pouring rain, but I had reporters come out from the Patriot News, Channel 27, Channel 43, and Channel 8 came at 5:00 p.m. for a live report.

Looking at the Capitol like the chained dog looks at the house.

Below is the statement I read at the conference:

I am Tamira Thayne, founder and CEO of Dogs Deserve Better, and **I have spent 52 days chained to a doghouse on these Capitol steps. That's one day for each week of the year Pennsylvania dogs spend chained in backyards,** suffering chewed up ears from flystrike in the summer heat, embedded collars from owners who fail to even notice the puppy has grown into a dog, frozen nights without so much as a flap on the door of their doghouse or a sliver of straw to warm the cold ground, and heatstroke when they can find not a patch of shade or a drop of water to cool them.

I could never say I've suffered as they have, for each night at 6:00 p.m. I returned to a hotel where I spent the next 14 hours before becoming a dog again.

I have endured many things out here, such as the pouring rain we're experiencing right now, and I've endured it repeatedly. I have worn no rain gear, used no umbrella, but have stayed wet for up to ten hours as do those dogs who cannot fit into their houses or have no house.

I created no false shade when it was over 100 degree heat index, even though I began to suffer heatstroke on two different occasions, experiencing headaches, nausea, and stomach aches before receiving a cold drink which helped me to recover.

I eschewed food while on the chain, and I drank sparingly much of the time.

Through all this I attempted to bring the suffering of Man's Best Friend to the legislators at the Capitol, legislators who may not have to witness this form of abuse on a daily basis due to living privileged lives in privileged settings.

Settings where they do not have to witness the daily suffering of the chained dog, and therefore do not understand how painful it is for the dog, for the kindly neighbors who have to witness the abuse, and for the children who are attacked by these same dogs that are not socialized with humans and become more and more territorial and aggressive.

During the short time I have been chained on the Capitol steps, three children in Pennsylvania made the papers from chained dog attacks. **The worst attack, on Alaha Crutchfield, 6, of McKeesport described her as being 'nearly scalped' by the dog who broke his chain to attack.**

The need for a tethering law is not going away; dogs and

children will continue to perish over the winter and into the spring, and we will be back next session to make sure meaningful tethering legislation is passed.

I apologize to the chained dogs of Pennsylvania on behalf of the state legislature, for they have once again ignored your plight despite the fact that I gave it my very all. I apologize to the people who have to live next door to a barking chained dog, and have to experience not only the aggravation of nightly noise when they are trying to sleep, but also the pain of knowing that dog is out there suffering and possibly dying in the extremes of hot and cold temperatures. And I apologize to the children and parents of mauled/injured children and the parents of children killed by chained dogs.

You will remain in my thoughts, and I implore you to stand with me next session to make these legislators understand that socializing our dogs with humans must be done on behalf of the children as well as the dogs.

Dogs enhance our lives and protect us everyday, from assisting us as seeing eye and therapy dogs, to protecting the public at airports, protecting police officers, and protecting our troops at war. It is ridiculous that the state of Pennsylvania cannot provide some basic protections from the cruel practice of continuous tethering.

Continuous tethering is passive cruelty and neglect. Continuous tethering is not as overtly obvious as someone beating a dog—but continuous tethering is as equally cruel. Pennsylvania must do something to protect the dogs and the children from the dangerous impacts of 24-7, 365 days a year tethering.

Most dogs who live for 11 years will spend over 96,000 hours on a chain, with little to no hope of ever attaining freedom. This is **96,000** too many. This abuse of our Best Friends must stop.

⚜

   I will be taking a tour of the Capitol tomorrow before I go home, as I've watched thousands of people go by me to take the tour since I've been chained at the bottom of the steps. Then I will go home, hug my dogs, and have dinner with my kids. I will clean my house (unless you want to volunteer?) and I will get back to work. **We have dogs to free!**

The Afterparty
Thoughts from 'the Other Side'

April 25, 2011

☾☉

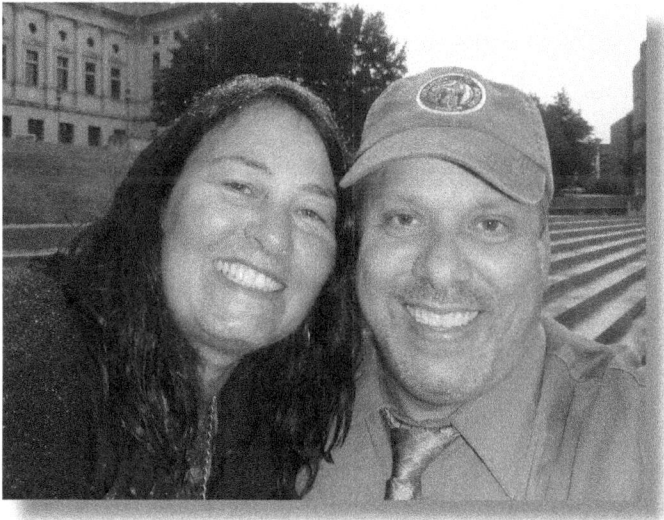

Joe and I at the very end. I was so happy to leave, but so sad for the dogs.

Six months have passed since I spent quality time with our Pennsylvania Senate and House leaders at the Capitol.

Too bad I still don't know their names or faces.

We already have two bills in play in the new session, which encourages me, for I believe animals bills are beginning to be taken more seriously in the good 'ol U. S. of A. We are also planning a one day Chain Off at my location on the Capitol steps this June 20, and I am hoping for and expecting at least 20 people with doghouses to join me for ten hours.

It really is a new day for dogs. For one woman to spend so much time, fail, and then come back with 20 more people sends a message to our legislators that she is not just acting alone, she is bringing a message that is supported by the people, a message that needs to be heard and acted upon.

I read Nelson Mandela's *Long Walk to Freedom* after my chaining, and gained some much-needed guidance and inspiration. The man endured so much for his people, spent decades in prison, and all the while never lost hope—even when all seemed lost, his years of work for naught.

The South African activists did repeated work shut downs that failed to bring change, people protested, activists overseas kept the story going, and yet it was still a long, hard siege before he and his people won.

As disappointed as I was that my comparatively small siege did nothing to bring change for Pennsylvania's dogs, reading Nelson's book helped me put in perspective that it was just one piece of the puzzle, just one brick thrown at a wall that needs continuous battering to break it down.

One would think a bill ensuring better treatment for dogs in Pennsylvania would be an easy sell, but going up against the old, entrenched thinking is tough.

In fact, I would postulate that not only are the dogs of Pennsylvania in chains, but the legislature of Pennsylvania is in chains as well, only their chains are even more binding and restrictive. Fear of pissing off the old guard and losing their high money campaign donors keeps them in tow with groups having both more power and more cash. In the end, staying in office is what matters to them, so they rarely take the steps that our society needs to advance as human beings until it is forced upon them.

We must be that force.

I know we can finish this. Anti-tethering legislation is the wave of the present, and the more we press for it, the more we make the phone calls and the more we show up for events, the sooner the dogs will have their day.

I truly can't do it alone. These dogs need ALL of us.

Promise this baby who still waits for a law that you will be there for him. Doesn't he deserve it?

Arguments
Against Anti-Tethering Legislation

by **Mike Romberger**
Campaign Manager for Operation Fido's Freedom

ᏹᎧᎧ

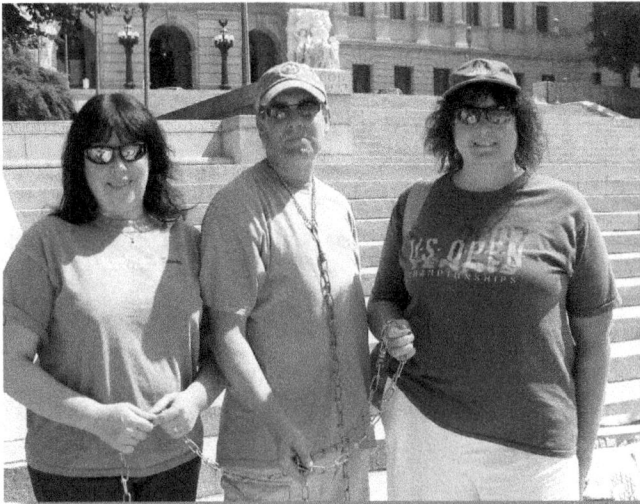

Mike Romberger, chained, middle, poses with more supporters

Since the OFF campaign started in August, I've heard numerous supporters call SB1435 a "no-brainer." A no-brainer implies that the benefits of this bill are so obvious that the bill can pass without debate. With less than a week until the end of the session, maybe this is not a no-brainer after all. We need to continue to educate the public so it becomes a no-brainer for the voting public. I'd like to address some of the reasons that I've heard from opponents of the bill.

"My dogs like it outside."

This is always one of those statements that needs some clarifying. I normally can break these folks into three categories. The first group is afraid SB1435 will take away their ability to tie out their dogs for 5-minute potty breaks. SB1435 prohibits tethering from 10:00 pm to 6:00 am, but still allows tethering up to 15 minutes during the prohibited times. This bill will not affect dog owners in this group. However, there are several reasons not to put your dog outside unsupervised and I'll get to that in a minute.

The second group consists of owners who have dogs that rush to get outside. Sure, the vast majority of dogs enjoy being outside. The dogs enjoy the freedom that an open sky brings. These owners fear that this bill will prevent their dogs from lying outside on a pleasant spring day. This bill will not prevent this type of behavior. The problem with this attitude is that many of these owners take this one-step too far. Many of these owners may believe that it is appropriate to chain their dogs while they are at work.

I can tell you from experience that on a nice day, my dogs take more coaxing to come inside. If it is raining or too hot they are begging to be in the house. Even in cold weather, my mountain dogs agree that the house is the preferred spot. Kobelt, et al, (2007) discovered that dogs left alone in the backyard spent most of the time looking in the door or at a gate. There is no doubt that dogs enjoy being outside, but only for limited amounts of time. They would rather be in the house or with their humans (Kos, 2005; Tuber, et al, 1996).

The last group of people that say "my dog likes it outside" tend to be chronic chainers. They may not be currently chaining their dog but they feel that 24/7 is not only appropriate but the preferred lifestyle for dogs. From my experience, the majority of these owners had chained dogs as children. This is the cycle that we need to break. As adults, it is difficult to believe that our parents were wrong. We believe that the advice our parents gave us was sound and something to pass to our children. Most chainers speak of their chained childhood pet with great admiration. In many cases, Mom or Dad simply said the Lucky preferred living outside and that is why we chained Lucky outside. I can provide all the scientific proof in the world, but Mom and Dad can never be wrong in their eyes.

There are more practical reasons not to leave a dog outside unsupervised. Dogs that are considered "yard dogs" (i.e. not allowed in house) are less likely to see a veterinarian, be licensed, or be spayed/neutered (Shore et al, 2006). Outside dogs are not vaccinated against rabies as often as indoor dogs. This puts chained dogs at much greater risk for rabies since wild animals have more access to these dogs.

There are also dangers from Class B dealers. These dealers obtain animals for research laboratories. They typically obtain free animals from newspapers and Craigslist. However, Class B dealers and their agents are not beyond taking unsupervised pets from the owners' yards. A great parody site demonstrates the need to better control Class B dealers (http://ibuystrays.com/).

"I work at night"

One of the problems with SB1435 is that it gives dog owners the impression that it is fine to chain dogs from 6:00 a.m. to 10:00 p.m. I now have heard complaints that SB1435 unfairly targets people that work at night. It goes something like this, "If people that work a traditional day shift can chain a dog, why does this bill target those that work a night shift?"

At first, I thought this was just a one-off complaint. Then I heard it from several sources including Senator Brubaker. To say the least, this one really baffles me. It probably directly affects far less than 1% of all PA dogs, yet the politicians point to this as a reason not to bring SB1435 up for a vote.

My response is simple: Become responsible for your pet. In all honesty, I can almost understand the 24/7 chainers. That sort of chaining is part of a culture and breaking a cultural mindset is difficult to break. However, I cannot understand the folks that have a need to chain their dog while at work for 8 to 10 hours. To me, these owners are as unwilling to deal with the pet as the 24/7 chainers.

As a certified dog trainer, I know it is possible to overcome most common problems that may lead to putting a dog outside. These reasons tend to include house soiling and destructive chewing. In my opinion, these are issues that are easy to control. Chaining a dog outside is just the path of least resistance. Dogs Deserve Better (http://www.dogsdeservebetter.org/) is more than happy to provide assistance to moving a dog indoors. If more dedicated training is needed, the APDT (http://apdt.com/) can recommend a trainer to help.

I have also heard that some dog owners are afraid they will be cited if they get home after 10:00 p.m. Again, this is a fairly weak argument for opposing SB1435. As was discussed in the previous section, it is dangerous for dogs to be outside unsupervised especially at night. It is better for the owners to hire a dog walker when these situations occur. We need to adjust the mindset that a dog must be chained outside when the owner is not home and to provide practical alternatives to chaining.

"My dog is used for protection"

In most cases, dog owners mean that a chained dog will scare off potential thieves. This I can understand. However, I would think a dog inside the home is a far better deterrent than one chained 50 feet from the home. I will not disagree that a chained dog will bark if an intruder comes to the home. This same dog, though, will bark at a squirrel, the neighbors, his family, a jogger running past, or almost anything that breaks up the monotony of the day. It will not take long for the dog's barking to be ignored or, worse yet, the dog's barking to be suppressed through aversive methods. I always relate this to a car alarm. Car alarms are so prevalent and go off so unexpectedly that people rarely pay attention to them. The same goes for the barking "guard" dog.

SB1435 does allow for chained dogs to protect agricultural property. I find this just as silly. As I stated before a chained dog is not going to stop intruders on a farm, especially a large one.

The more rational solution would be to let the dog roam free; however, farm owners fear that a loose dog would harass or kill livestock. Motion sensing lights tend to be more effective, cover more ground, and are less expensive than a dog.

There are rare cases where the dog is chained so it may physically harm potential intruders. These are disasters waiting to happen. Dogs like this are more likely to bite a mail carrier or a child than to ever stop or capture a thief. Dog bites are already the cause of one-third of all homeowner's insurance claims (Insurance Information Institute, 2010). Any owner that would use a dog in this way would have difficulty proving they were not negligent. Unfortunately, there is typically a death sentence for a biting dog in these instances.

"The government can't tell me what to do."

No one enjoys the perception of government interference. However, this argument simply makes little sense but is the hardest to overcome. Anyone who uses this argument tends to be defensive about chaining. In any situation where you imply someone is wrong, the recipient will immediately create a defensive reaction. It cannot be helped, for most people it has become a reflex. The representatives with Dogs Deserve Better can tell you that they've had more success with owners when they did not create a defensive atmosphere. I've lost many battles by choosing the wrong approach.

With that being said, I still believe this Bill is the right way to go. While DDB can save one dog at a time from life on a chain, this bill would protect thousands of dogs almost immediately.

The biggest disappointment with the government interference argument is that it implies that dogs are merely property. Those that cite government interference see their dogs as property and not as companions. (If they did, would the dog be chained in the farthest corner of the property?)

I don't know if it will ever be possible to reason with these owners or if we should even try. These dogs need the most protection and thus the reason for SB1435. SB1435 has similarities to domestic violence and child protective services (CPS) laws. These laws protect the innocent even though the innocent comprise a relatively small percentage of the population. It is truly ironic that in the 1870s, prosecutors used animal abuse laws to protect children from abuse since no CPS laws were in place. Now we have come full circle. We are now asking that a law be put into place that will help dogs receive the mental and physical stimulation they require. It is a shame that we live in a society where providing food, water, and shelter are considered the minimum responsibility for both parents and dog owners. While we cannot legislate compassion and empathy, we can make those understand the consequences for not protecting the innocent.

Yes, I consider the passing of SB1435 a no-brainer and if you read this far, so do you. At this point in the legislative session, it is doubtful that SB1435 will pass. It is up to us to continue the fight into the next legislative session. Keep contacting your legislator—in PA or in other states that allow 24/7 chaining. Remind them that you vote (you vote, don't you?), and this is something that is important to you. I can only hope that this document will help you counteract the naysayers and the chainers. A dog on the end of a chain cannot count on their owners to be their voice, they need you.

References

Insurance Information Institute (2010). Dog Bite Liability. Retrieved from http://www.iii.org/media/hottopics/insurance/dogbite/.

Kobelt, A.; Hemsworth, P.; Barnett, J.; Coleman, G.; Butler, K. (2007). The behaviour of Labrador retrievers in suburban backyards: The relationships between the backyard environment and dog behaviour. Applied Animal Behaviour Science, 106, 70-84.

Kos, U. (2005). Do dogs show preferences for certain types of environmental enrichments. International Society for Animal Hygiene, Volume 2. (pp. 479-483). Warsaw, Poland.

Shore, E.R., Riley, M.L., Douglas, D.K. (2006). Pet owner behaviors and attachment to yard versus house dogs. Anthrozoos 19, 325–334.

Tuber, D. S.; Hennessy, M. B.; Sanders, S.; Miller, J. A. (1996) Behavioral and glucocorticoid responses of adult domestic dogs (Canis familiaris) to companionship and social separation. Journal of Comparative Psychology, 110, 103–108.

Testimonials
from Newfound Friends

Cathie MacArthur and Deb Smith

ळॐ

Cathie MacArthur points out that the cruelty must stop.

"From the time I took that first glass of water over to you, I knew we had to be friends, and I wanted to help you in any way possible to remain strong during your chaining on the Capitol steps.

"I witnessed you experience so much emotion, the commitment, days of happiness, days of silence and sorrow, days of utter frustration and anger, and the final day of knowing you completed a very important task. Love you, my friend."

Deb Smith, chained and wearing her Doogie shirt.

"The chaining of dogs has long been a major source of anxiety for me—long before I ever heard of Tamira Ci Thayne and Dogs Deserve Better. When I first became aware of her organization's efforts, I was overjoyed and so thankful. And, when I saw Tami's photo with a chain around her neck at a Chain Off event, I thought 'I wanna do that, too!'

"I finally got the opportunity on July 4, 2010 when I joined Justin Strawser and his mom, Cherie Smith on their property for DDB's annual Chain-Off event—where we endured all that the chained dogs endure, including biting ants. I was honored to meet up with Tami at the Capitol steps as much as possible during her lengthy 2010 vigil. And from now on, I will proudly wear a chain collar at any event—even if I only plant one seed, to help educate the public about the inherent cruelty of chaining Man's Best Friend. I am amazed at Tami's perseverance, and proud to count her among my friends."

The Aftermath
Thoughts from 'the Long Game'

December 4, 2017

☙❧

Senator Andrew Dinniman hugs me during the Chain Off 2011,
while holding the first edition of Capitol in Chains. *Senator Dinniman*
was a co-sponsors of SB1453, the bill we were working to pass.
[All photos this section courtesy Redheaded Ninja Photography.]

Finally, finally, finally—almost seven years after my chaining campaign—a state law limiting chaining passed in the state of Pennsylvania. *I could cry just typing these words.*

In June of 2017, Pennsylvania passed a comprehensive animal care package, which benefits chained dogs by prohibiting tethering for more than nine hours a day, and—even better—allows only 30 minutes or less in temperatures below 32 degrees or above 90 degrees.

Nationwide, as of this writing, there were at least 104 cities and counties that completely BANNED the chaining of dogs altogether. *Not one of these is in Pennsylvania.* However, there are now over 189 cities and counties nationwide that limit tethering, **with five of these cities or counties reporting in from Pennsylvania!** *Now that the state law has passed, towns and cities in Pennsylvania with laws limiting chaining will need to ensure that their laws are at least as strict as the state law. If not, the state law will supercede them.*

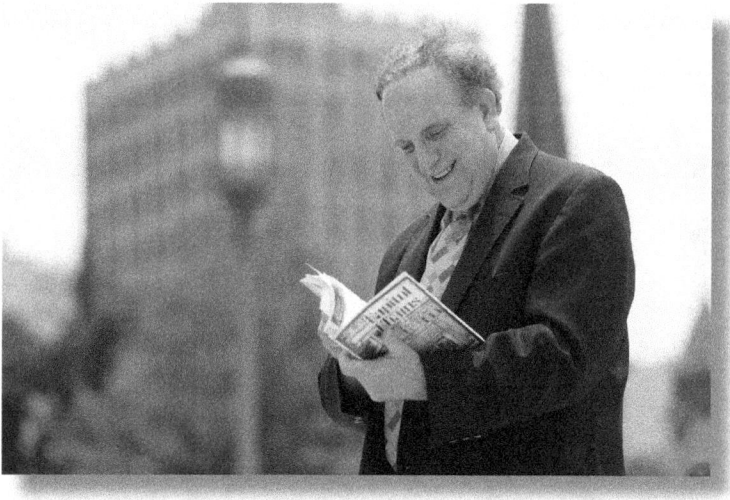

Senator Andrew Dinniman reading the first edition of Capitol in Chains.

When I chained myself to a doghouse on the Pennsylvania State Capitol steps in 2010, my steadfast dream—the one that kept me going—was that this day would come for chained dogs. It didn't happen then, but now, in 2017, animal advocates and concerned citizens who came together to make this dream a reality can lay this gift at the feet of the chained dogs, finally presenting them with the justice they deserve. I, for one, couldn't be happier about it.

When I chained in Harrisburg in 2010, Hazelton was the ONLY Pennsylvania town with anti-chaining legislation. Now others have joined in. In fact, the city of Harrisburg passed an anti-tethering law in 2013, which states: "Dogs may not be tethered for longer than it takes the owner or responsible person to complete a temporary task for which the dog must be restrained. Dogs may not be left outside unattended in severe weather."

The Harrisburg city chaining ordinance was headed up by Brad Koplinski, the very same council member who passed a resolution urging the state to pass the anti-chaining law while I was chained in front of the Capitol.

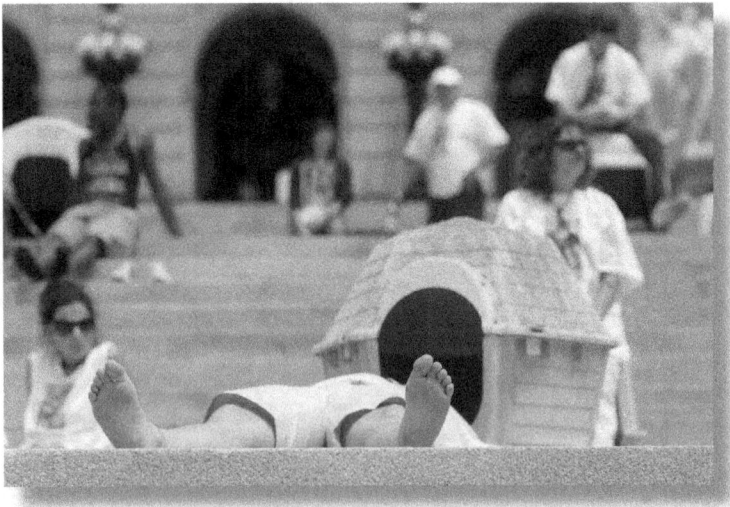

Doghouses and activists covered the Capitol steps during Chain Off 2011.

He was incredibly moved by what I had undertaken on behalf of the dogs, and once we failed at the state level (again), Brad took matters into his own hands at the city level, getting the job done. Philly Dawg blogger Amy Worden wrote: "Koplinski said that since the state had failed to pass a statewide tethering ban he decided to move forward with a city ordinance. Perhaps we can put pressure on the statehouse," he said.

Brad's success on behalf of chained dogs illustrates that we never know how our actions move others. These folks can then act in their own spheres of influence and create an ever-expanding ripple effect. Even though we may feel disappointed without an out and out victory, we can still make a difference, and the sacrifice is still worthwhile. I truly believe that.

At this point, it would be remiss of me not to say "*Bite Me*" to the anonymous online person who called my 54-day protest an "epic fail." Oh, and natty natty boo boo.

40 people chained to doghouses on the Capitol steps in June 2011. Can you imagine?

Special Addition: The Capitol Doghouse Wedding

June 20, 2011

The wedding party, chained to doghouses, with the exception of Joe's brother-in-law.
[All photos this section by Redheaded Ninja Photography.]

I'm a girl (fine, an OLDER girl), and I'd wager most people who will read this book or this section of the book will also be of the female persuasion. Therefore, I feel it's my duty as a fellow romanticist to regale you with the details of the Doghouse

Wedding Joe and I held on the steps of the Pennsylvania State Capitol building. After all, we women DO LOVE a good wedding!

*Joe and I getting married—while chained to doghouses—
on the Capitol steps at the 2011 Chain Off.*

So here's the scoop on how the Doghouse Wedding came to be.

I'd always wanted to be married in an unusual way. This would be my fourth wedding (hey, I never claimed to be good at marriage) so I had already done the traditional marriage thing. Twice. And the other was a justice of the peace ceremony.

As I sat for days on end staring at the Capitol building—mostly bored out of my mind—it became all too easy to picture my fancy Doghouse Wedding on those very Capitol steps.

I couldn't imagine a cooler way to combine raising awareness for an important cause AND getting hitched.

Trouble was, Joe wasn't feelin' the same overwhelming coolness vibes that I was. As an introvert, the very thought of being chained to a doghouse in a tuxedo—in front of a bunch of people and in a very public place—freaked him out. He gently, but resolutely, refused to get married chained to a doghouse on the Capitol steps.

I was terribly saddened and disappointed about it, even though I understood his feelings. He tried talking me into other, more traditional, avenues like a destination or beach wedding, but my heart just wasn't in it. I couldn't consider it.

I also knew I couldn't make my—admittedly weird—dream his too. And I didn't know how to fix the situation.

I really thought Joe was 'the one.' After 45 years, I had met the man who truly felt like HOME to me; the man who stood by me through thick and thin, encouraged but didn't baby me, and let me go into crazy or potentially dangerous situations in rescue and activist work without trying to scare or shame me out of it.

He respected me as an equal partner, and didn't overprotect or control, as many men would have done in his shoes. He got me, even though we were very different people from each other.

I wasn't willing to relinquish my dream of getting married chained to a doghouse, and he wasn't willing to relinquish his notion of getting married in a more traditional fashion.

We were at an impasse.

Our first discussion on the topic was in January of 2011, and I wanted to get married during Chain Off that June or July; this left me six months to change his mind, if such a thing were possible. In reality, at that point, I had just resigned myself to not getting married anytime soon.

We went about our daily lives, Joe living and working in Virginia, and me working for the chained dogs from my home in Pennsylvania. We were still engaged, and continued to spend time together as much as we possibly could.

Joe's sons Taylor and Garrett were troopers about it. Unfortunately, my son Rayne was in basic training at the time, so he missed the wedding. Perhaps being chained to a doghouse would have been preferable to the hell of basic training? I think so.

We skirted the subject for the next four months, but I started planning a Chain Off for the Pennsylvania Capitol steps in June of 2011. In April we were discussing the event, and I jokingly said to Joe, "Well, we'd better get your tux ordered then. We're running out of time."

He said, "Yeah, I guess you're right. Let's do it." I was floored! Now, mind you, I'm sure he still wasn't jumping for joy about it, but he had agreed to my idea, and he was doing it because he loved me. That meant a lot.

I was beyond ecstatic. "Are you sure?" I asked; I didn't want to start planning and then have him back out.

"Yes, I'm sure, honey. I love you, and I want you to be happy. So what do we do to get this party started?"

Planning for the event then took a decidedly different direction with the addition of the wedding!

I'd been doing Chain Offs since 2004, and I knew it was always difficult—if not damn near impossible—to get people to come chain up with me. Not only have we become a more virtual society, but most people work one or more jobs, and what little free time they have they aren't too keen on spending in tortuous ways.

I get that.

Finally, we're free. And, we look to be happy to be married. That's something!

But now I had an ace up my sleeve! I could lure them into Chain Off with a wedding prize at the end. Mwahaha!

I don't know about you, but I love myself a good wedding. I don't even consider myself a girly girl, but if I had a chance to stand up for the animals AND watch an animal activist wedding at the end of the day? Count me in.

I announced the wedding a month in advance in our e-news, and all our DDB supporters—plus friends and family, of course—were invited...anyone who wanted to come out and chain with us all day at the Chain Off was welcome, or they could even just come by for the wedding.

Our list of chainees immediately doubled! (I'm brilliant like that.)

Melissa Swauger brought Sonny to the wedding, a dog I was blessed to free from the chain. He was adopted by Melissa and her hubby and lived a blessed life.

The wedding was amazing, and beautiful (I cried), and even filmed by a local news crew who put it on their website. I'd do it all over again if I could, and do it even better the second time!

One of my favorite parts of the wedding to remember today was the "blooper reel." First, I tripped on my gown going down the steps, but luckily Joe was there and caught me, so that didn't end in complete disaster.

Then, one of my Air Force friends, Mark, was performing our ceremony for us. He'd forgotten to print out new vows, so was using sheets from a previous wedding he'd performed. When it came time for Joe's vows, he mistakenly called him Scott, the name of the previous groom. "Do you Scott, take..."

Without missing a beat, Joe turned and looked around at the wedding guests, calling out "Scott? Scott?" It was awesome! I laughed so hard, and I still smile today when I think of that moment.

Our wedding "blooper reel" highlights two of the reasons I married that man...He catches me when I fall, AND he makes an awkward situation better by finding the humor instead of the humiliation. I loved it.

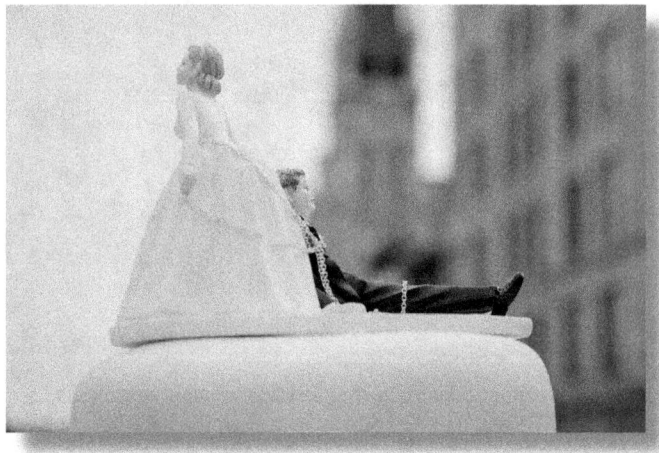

We had a little fun with the cake topper, too. Not only is the bride dragging her groom to the doghouse wedding, she has him chained to her as well. Ha!

Joe's joke about the doghouse wedding has been the same since the day he said "I'll do it."

"A guy starting his marriage off in the doghouse...Well, he can only move up from there..."

[I wouldn't be so sure about that, buddy! We women know.]

The History
of Chain Off, 2004-2014

YEAR ONE: JULY 3-4, 2004

☙❧

Me chained at the first-ever Chain Off in 2004, State College, Pennsylvania.

In early 2004, I got the idea to chain myself to a doghouse as an awareness campaign for chained dogs. I discussed "my crazy idea" with two local activist friends in State College, Pennsylvania—Terri Bunge and Amy Smith—who loved it and volunteered to help me. The two women proved to be crucial to the campaign, completely arranging the first-ever Chain Off, and bringing in media interviews and lots of support for the cause.

Snowball was chained to this house for his whole life.

I lived chained to a doghouse in State College, Pennsylvania for 33 hours July 3-4, 2004, moving to three different locations throughout the day and night. The goal was to bring aware-ness to our cause, and push to free Snowball, a dog who had been chained for at least 12 years near a Highway Pizza in State College. Many people over the years had tried to get help for him in his miserable plight, but since there were no laws to pro-tect him, calls for humane action fell on deaf ears.

Advance press in this case served to be both a blessing and a curse, because it alerted the owners to our plans. They moved Snowball before me and my team could get there to set up in front of his home. Snowball never returned to the area, and rumors circulated that they took the poor guy to another town where he died at the end of his chain. So sorry, Snowball!

I created an online diary of my 33 hours on the chain; an excerpt reads as follows:

"In the peaceful moments before the city wakes, I have time to think and feel. I am at one with Snowball, and I think to myself, 'Snowball and I are going to write a little more.' I give that some thought, and feel suddenly terrified and sad that maybe he doesn't KNOW I'm with him, doesn't even know he's not alone. Maybe he can't feel my oneness of spirit. I want to cry and I do.

"It's so unfair to these dogs that people treat them with so little respect. Dogs save people's lives, they alert them to seizures, help the handicapped. I sob for their pain. I can see clearly that I denied the inhumanity of my condition from the start of my chaining. I didn't want to feel that humiliation.

"I remember now that when I first snapped the chain onto my collar, I felt a moment of shame and victimization. I quickly squelched it because I knew I had to be strong for the dogs and interact with all those who came out to see me. Now I remember.

"I am overwhelmed with sadness and anguish. I haven't broken down like this in a long time; I'm always so busy, there's no time for such things. My body heaves with my sobbing. This is SO NOT RIGHT! Why can't they see it?"

⊙⊙

Amandah Povilitus, 17 and still in high school with a full-time job as a restaurant supervisor, made time to represent Dogs Deserve Better and the chained dogs at the Lackawanna County Stadium in Moosic, PA for 8 hours Sunday, July 4th. 87 people signed two letters apiece, one to her county's state senator and one to the state representative.

*Amandah Povilitus bravely chains by herself
at a public event in the very first Chain Off.*

YEAR TWO: JULY 2-3, 2005

☙❧

I once again lived chained to a doghouse for 33 hours July 2-3, 2005 in State College, Pennsylvania as part of the Dogs Deserve Better Chain Off event.

I was joined in the second year by four others across the country—Monica Kinley-Kuhn and Sam Hogenaur in Richmond, Indiana; Dan Paden in Richmond, Virginia; and Amandah Povilitus in Lackawanna, Pennsylvania. Each of the four wrote about their experiences, and they were summed up by Dan this way: "The small time that I spent chained recently lent me more empathy for tethered dogs than did my prior meetings with hundreds of these neglected animals combined."

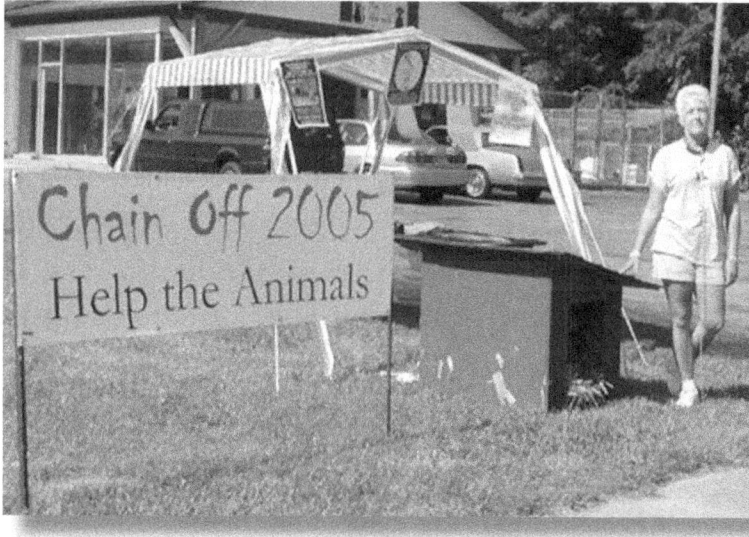

Monica Kinley-Kuhn in Indiana, chaining up for her first time.

YEAR THREE: JULY 1-15, 2006

For the 2006 Chain Off, we did the coolest thing—we held a contest, with participants chaining up to doghouses for the long haul; the person who stayed the longest won a new car!

If you lived in the Johnstown or Altoona, Pennsylvania area, you could not have missed footage or highlights of 2006's Chain Off Contest. Local coverage was phenomenal, with Channel Six coming out five or six times, as well as all the local papers doing preview and update stories. The Altoona Mirror printed a full page photo spread on the first Friday, unheard-of from them any-time previously. Publisher Jim Lauffer of Mainline Newspapers ran photos and updates of the event at least four times, and was out there encouraging our contestants on an almost daily basis. His mother even cooked them a vegetarian pasta meal! Total Pennsylvania coverage was 35-40 pieces. Nationwide we garnered a total of 65-70 pieces of press from this one event!

The contest was an amazing victory for chained dogs, as we were able to reach so many of the nation's citizens with the message that chaining just doesn't cut it. But, for one dog in particular, the contest directly saved her from life on the chain.

As soon as Don McKendree got off his chain, he went home and unchained his dog.

One of our contestants, Don McKendree, had a dog named Nikki living chained at his home. When Don first chained up, it was all about the prize for him, a new Chevy Aveo. When he wrote in his notebook each day, he wrote about mundane things such as the weather or the food. But as time went on, his entries changed. As Don spent days on the chain—using a port-a-potty, sleeping on the chain in all kinds of weather, forbidden to talk to fellow contestants—he underwent a deep metamorphosis of the spirit. He cried as he told me he couldn't believe what he'd subjected his dog to. He was heartsick over it.

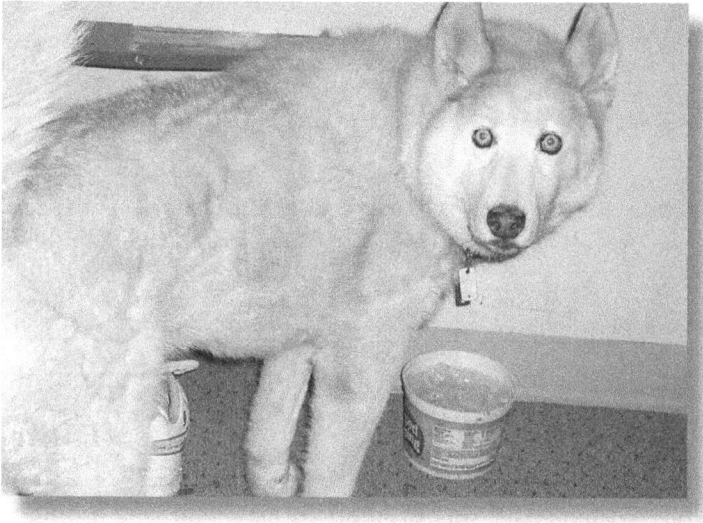

Nikki inside, proof that we were chain-ging lives for the better with our activism!

Don vowed that Nikki would never live chained again. Immediately after the event, he went home and freed Nikki, taking her into his home and family! We met him at Lowe's the next week to contribute to his fence fund for her . . . but Don paid for much of the fencing himself, because he wanted her to have a very large chain link fenced area with a doggie door so she could have the utmost freedom.

He also pledged to take action for other chained dogs he saw in his area. He'd become an advocate for life.

Aija Gillman being interviewed by a local TV station. Note the port-a-potties. No contestant was allowed to leave the chain for any reason or they were disqualified.

Our Grand Prize winner of a new Chevy Aveo was Aija Gillman, 18, from Pinckneyville, Illinois. Aija hung in there for 13 days, despite all the odds stacked against her: she missed her friends, she hated the food, and she just wanted to go home. But she stuck it out and proved to have what it takes to drive home the Big Prize!

In addition to our contest in 2006, eight others raised awareness for chain dogs by holding Chain Offs in Maine, Indiana, Ohio, and Pennsylvania. Erin Blaize, of Maine, wrote this of her event: "It was quite an experience. I was very bored most of the time but I knew that it wouldn't be forever. I did feel very secluded and alone. I could hear my husband and nephews playing in the pool, and it was awful...I so wanted to join them. I think I can somewhat understand how a chained dog feels. When I heard my husband coming I was very excited at the prospect of a little attention. It was strange to feel that way. I see people all the time and usually welcome the chance to be alone for a little while but I guess that is something I've taken for granted."

Lois Rose, chained for the dogs of Ohio in 2006.

YEAR FOUR: JUNE 30-JULY 30, 2007

๑๛

In 2007 our Chain Off participation increased exponentially, for a total of 108 people in 37 states! It was fantabulous. We had momentum going from the previous year's contest which was exciting to watch; people were wanting to get in on the action, be part of the solution. The event was called "Unchain the 50," with the goal being to get a Chain Off going in all 50 states. I must say, coming in at 37 states was not too shabby!

By this time I'd realized that we needed to move the big event each year in order to garner media attention. When you repeat the same event in the same place year after year, you become a non-entity to the media, making it harder to accomplish the task of spreading the word about chaining without their interest. But moving to a different state and different media market sparks fresh interest and a greater chance of media attention.

We traveled to Atlanta, Georgia, for the East Coast event, where we had 15 people chained to doghouses in the stifling heat of Piedmont Park. We spent 29 hours chained between the park venue and area rep Pam Cheatham's field, since the park wouldn't allow us to overnight there. (You can imagine the logistics of that move and then back again! Not fun.)

2007 Atlanta chainees. Bored, hot, and miserable.

There were seven people chained in Washington State for our West Coast "Unchain the 50," and people scattered all over the country and into Canada, with groups as large as 10 in Tennessee and Virginia. In addition to the four states already mentioned, there were participants in the following states: Arizona, Arkansas, California, Colorado, Connecticut, Delaware, Florida, Hawaii, Illinois, Indiana, Kansas, Kentucky, Louisiana, Maine, Maryland, Michigan, Minnesota, Mississippi, Missouri, Nebraska, New Jersey, New Mexico, New York,

North Carolina, Ohio, Pennsylvania, Rhode Island, South Carolina, Texas, Utah, Vermont, Wisconsin, and Wyoming. Can you believe it? It was amazing.

I posted video of our chainees from Atlanta on my youtube channel at youtube.com/tammyddb, and Rhonda Sims summed it up best when she said, "It must be really sad for dogs on chains...We have an end, and they don't. We have people around us, they don't."

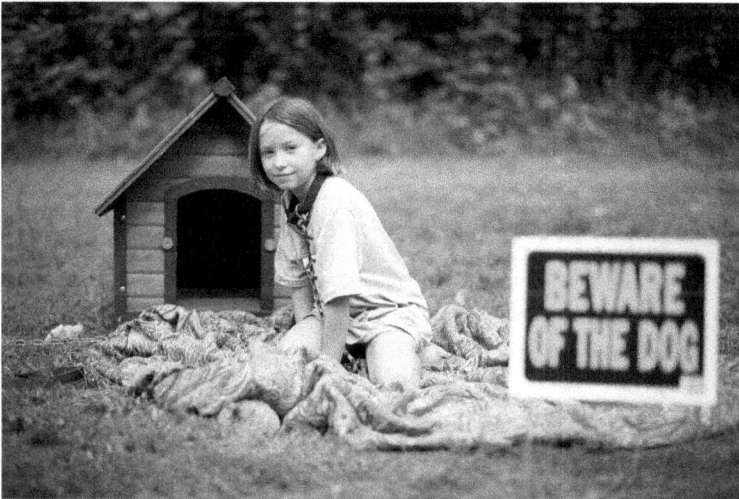

My daughter, Brynnan Grimes, chained in Atlanta, June 30, 2007. Don't worry, she begged to do it, AND she was allowed to get off her chain whenever she wanted! But she stayed the whole time, making her chain long enough to come sit on my lap when she felt like it. Photo credit: Jan Fields.

It proved to be our best year yet for media attention. We estimated 150-200 different media hits via TV or newspaper, with three Associated Press articles which were picked up and syndicated across the country and the world. We found the Seattle AP article in both France and England! It was a good year for the chained dog issue.

I wrote the following in my journal from that Chain Off: "I remember in last year's contest—where the chainees lived as long as 13 days chained to a doghouse—that they were so eager for companionship that if we came near them they would all but grab us and tackle us to get some attention. And if one contestant was doing something around his/her area, they all watched intently and then wrote about it in their journals later. I feel the same way about Kelly and I watching Dawn and Gordon assembling her sun umbrella. At that moment that single happening became our world. *And people wonder why chained dogs jump and annoy them when they come to feed them each evening?* They are living for that one single moment of the day. Heartbreaking and pitiful!"

2008 Chicago chainees survive thunderstorms, a night of rain, and even HAIL.

YEAR FIVE: JUNE 30-JULY 30, 2008

☉☉

In 2008, we took the main Chain Off to Chicago, Illinois, more specifically the Page County Fairgrounds. We had 13 people chained at the event, with another 72 participating in 23 other states, including Arizona, Arkansas, California, Delaware, Florida, Georgia, Idaho, Indiana, Kentucky, Maryland, Michigan, New Jersey, New Mexico, New York, North Carolina, Ohio, Pennsylvania, South Carolina, Texas, Virginia, Washington, West Virginia, and Wyoming. Thanks to volunteer coordinators Susan Hartland, Cynthia Drobitsch, and Cara Wilson, there was an entire festival going on with booths and doggie agility contests—but of course we chainees only saw it in photos.

I love the irony of us being chained while the dogs had a blast. How paradoxical!

The weather at the event was the worst I'd yet encountered at any Chain Off. Thunderstorms rolled through off and on throughout the day, and we were even pummeled with hail during a particularly bad bout of storms. Those of us who could get into our doghouses huddled inside (with spiders and other bugs, yuk!), but many couldn't even fit into their houses, and had to tough it out outside. Then it rained much of the night, soaking through sleeping bags, and making sure we were as miserable as we could possibly be. I'll never forget it.

My most poignant memory of all my Chain Off experiences

came from the middle of the night in that park in a Chicago suburb. I was sleeping outside in a borrowed sleeping bag, and the rain just kept coming steadily down, until I could no longer deny that I was soaked and would have to crawl into my buggy, creepy doghouse for shelter.

The hail coming into my doghouse.

I got up to go to the bathroom to look for something that wasn't soaked to cover myself with (finding only paper towels), when I noticed chainee Kim Jayne and her sister sitting in the rain—with no cover—at 2:30 in the morning. I thought to myself, "there's no way those two poor girls will still be there in the morning."

But they were! When I asked Kim why she stayed when no one would have been the wiser if she snuck out, her response was "the dogs don't get to leave, no matter how miserable their lives are. There was no part of me that was giving up and walking away from that horrible night in the rain. I stayed for the dogs; if that was all I had to give, then I gave them my all."

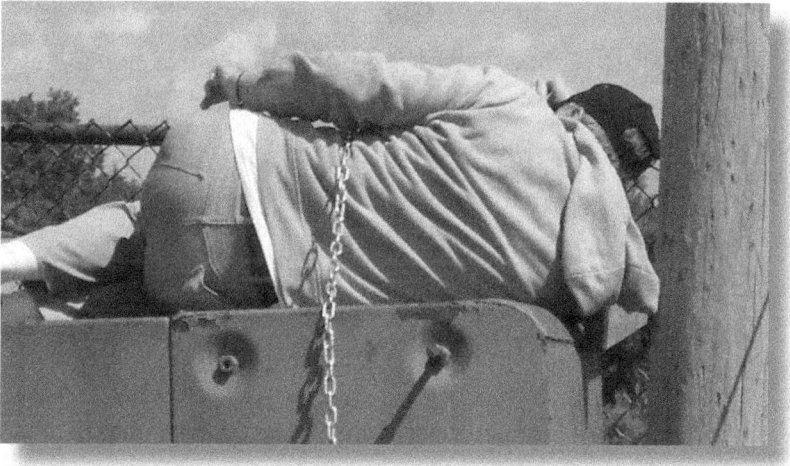

Chainee Gordon Bakalar, author of the below poem which I read at the event.

TOUGH LOVE

I am a dog with a story to tell
A dog on a chain, my life a living hell.

I was unlucky enough to be born in a "mill"
Though they passed new laws, it's probably there still.

I was born in a small wire pen
Along with my brothers, six of us kin.

We were not kept together for very long
Before taken to auction and sold for a song.

Sold to a pet store, my home a glass cage
I was one of those designer dogs, "all of the rage."

So again I was sold in about a week
Little did I know it was "up the creek."

I was bought for a Christmas present for the kids
But that didn't last long before I hit the skids.

At first it was a happy and playful time
I lived in a big house, everything was fine.

Played with two children, my master and his wife
This was the greatest, this was the life.

But then all of a sudden things got real hard
I was thrown outside to live in the yard.

Maybe it's because I do shed a little
Or once on the rug I did a little piddle.

No explanation and no reason why
All night alone I would whimper and cry.

When the sun came up I barked all day
But no one, not even the kids, came out to play.

I've grown a little older now living on a chain
They say I'm too big for the house, too much trouble to train.

This is my story, and my lament
I'm nothing more than a lawn ornament.

I've been waiting for my master for close to 15 years
Tied in the back yard, I choked back my tears.

I hope you think of me when you see a dog on a chain
And know that dog is lonely, hurting, and in pain.

Maybe you'll even stop a while and pat him on his head
Or just sit beside him and talk to him instead.

If you stay long enough to say a friendly word
It's sure to be a kindness that for years he's never heard.

\When you see a chained dog and know of his plight
You'll know in your heart and mind, it just ain't right.

By Gordon Bakalar

The chainees huddled for protection from the storm. Imagine the terror the dogs feel left out in extreme weather conditions! Most chained dogs I rescued had very bad storm anxiety. We experienced first-hand why that happens.

YEAR SIX: JUNE -JULY, 2009

⌾⌾

In 2009 we held our largest Chain Off, bringing in a whopping 120 volunteers who chained themselves to doghouses in at least 29 states, British Columbia, and Romania.

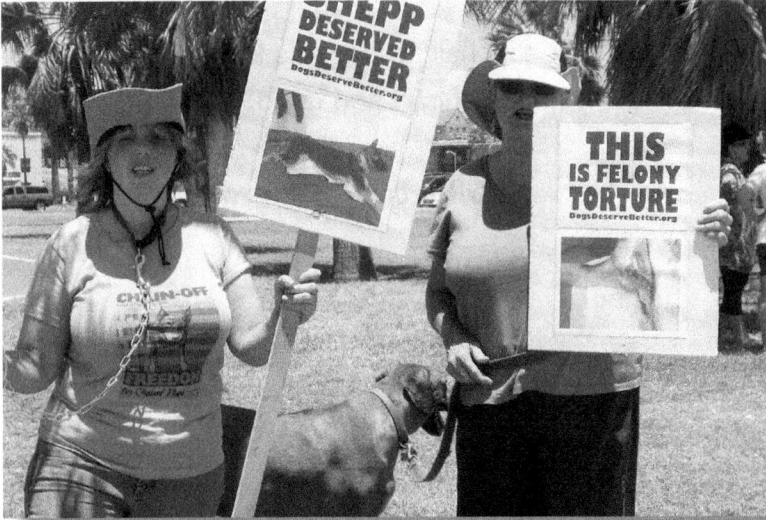

Volunteers in Corpus Christi, Texas, chained up and protested on poor Shepp's behalf.

I did three Chain Offs that year, first traveling to Corpus Christi, Texas, where a beautiful shepherd named Shepp died as a result of being starved and chained, with no ability to free himself to find food or help. He was rescued but he lost his fight for life four days later.

Activists around the world were understandably heartbroken and outraged at the suffering that poor dog had undergone, so our Chain Off in Corpus Christi was in a very public park along the beach highway, and focused on the lack of laws and justice for Shepp. While there, I attempted to confront his owners, but they refused to answer their door when I knocked. Probably for the best...would have probably led to another arrest for me!

Eric and Terri Bunge gear up for Chain Off 2009 in State College, Pennsylvania.

Then on July 4th I met back up with my Chain Off roots—Terri Bunge and Amy Smith—in State College, Pennsylvania, and we spent the day raising awareness for the sixth year in that location. It was wonderful! I missed those ladies.

There were also events held by many others in the following states and countries: Arizona, Arkansas, California, Connecticut, Florida, Georgia, Illinois, Indiana, Kentucky, Maryland, Michigan, Minnesota, Mississippi, Missouri, Montana, Nebraska, New Jersey, New Mexico, New York, North Carolina, Ohio, Tennessee, Virginia, Washington, West Virginia, Wisconsin, British Columbia, Canada, and Bucharest, Romania.

On July 11-12 we joined another anti-chaining group, PAWSitive Effects, that had formed in Simpsonville, South

Carolina after founder Mikael Hardy was a contestant at our Chain Off contest in 2006.

*Steve Cates, also known as The Duke of Elvis, sang the blues
from his doghouse in the town square of Greensville.*

There were at least 13 people chained over the two days in Greenville, South Carolina, and we were blessed to have a primo spot in the downtown section, in a square that everyone passed by for shopping and/or dining. Even if they didn't stop, we were seen and noticed by thousands of people during that weekend timeframe.

We overnighted at Mikael's farm, sleeping under the stars and sharing a beautiful evening of camaraderie while we were serenaded by The Duke of Elvis. The weather cooperated, and although we bore the immense sadness of our understanding of the effects of chaining on dogs, we didn't suffer the weather extremes they are often forced to endure.

Rhonda Sims giving an interview to the local news in Greensville, South Carolina.

We were even joined by Chain Off Barbie that year. My daughter sent Barbie along in her stead, since Brynnan couldn't come with me that year.

YEAR SEVEN: JUNE -JULY, 2010

∽∾

2010 was an unusual Chain Off year, with a "Chain Off in Twitter" campaign from my doghouse in Florida, a Chain Off doghouse parade float in Kentucky, and two other large Chain Offs in both New Mexico and Texas. Altogether we logged a total of 89 people chained in 23 states plus Guam and British Columbia: Arkansas, California, Colorado, Delaware, Florida, Illinois, Indiana, Kansas, Kentucky, Maine, Maryland, Missouri, New Jersey, New Mexico, New York, Ohio, Pennsylvania, South Carolina, Texas, Virginia, Washington, Wisconsin, and Wyoming.

My favorite Chain Off photo of all time! So awesome. Joe, who was my boyfriend at the time (and now hubby) fell asleep on top of his doghouse at the Alachua, Florida Chain Off, trying to avoid the biting ants. Just another drawback of being a chained dog. You can't get away from any insects that colonize your area!

In Alachua, Florida, we were scheduled to have 18 chainees,

and only eight showed up, which was disappointing. We also had no media for the event. This was in the early days of Twitter, so I did a "Chain Off in Twitter" campaign, where I tweeted the haps or funny or thought-provoking things every hour or so. Some samples are as follows:

Sitting on my igloo to avoid the antbites. However the rounded design isn't conducive to sitting. Punchbug; hit yourself for me. 2:32 PM Jul 3rd

I just have to say it: if you were committed to show up here to chain and u broke a nail and had to stay home I have one word for you: LA-ME 2:41 PM Jul 3rd

I know what you're thinking. Yeah, I'm kinda a dork.

Dark clouds heading my way. Will I have to crawl inside my doghouse? Stay tuned. 3:01 PM Jul 3rd

We're lucky. It's been hot, but not Africa hot. 3:26 PM Jul 3rd

Visited the orange port-a-john for the first time, a record in dehydration. Most excited to see hand sanitizer. It's the little things. 3:42 PM Jul 3rd

For the overnight we were down to three—me, Joe, and Rhonda Sims, one of my most-faithful Chain Off supporters. We were eaten alive by red ants, and Joe stayed up most of the night because he was afraid we were vulnerable to humans looking to steal or harm us. In short, we found ourselves in as tenuous a situation as the chained dogs do each and every day of their lives. It was humbling.

The doghouse parade float made by Kentucky DDB Rep Tammi Kinman Ruppert and her volunteers. They were seen by thousands of people. Very creative solution!

In Kentucky, DDB Rep Tammi Kinman Ruppert and her volunteers had come up with a brilliant plan to ensure they were seen; they took their Chain Off mobile! They built a parade float and joined a 4th of July parade, where they took turns chaining to the doghouse and passing out information and dog biscuits.

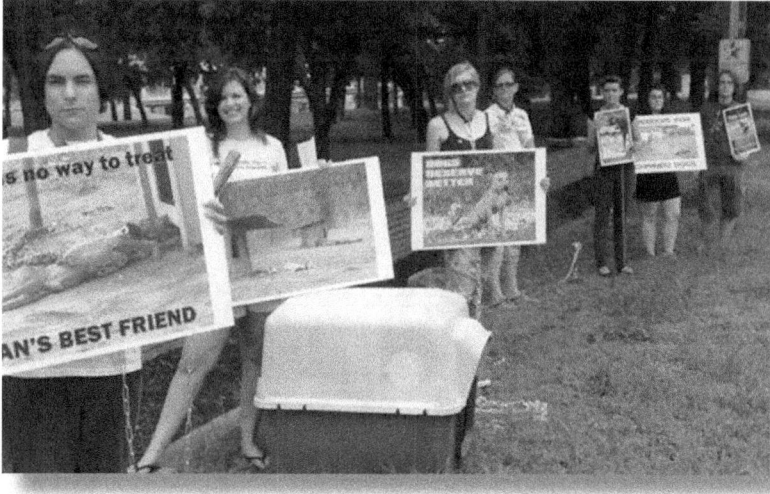

In Dallas, Texas, DDB Rep Niloofar Asgharian and her volunteers chained up next to a busy road, making quite the statement for all who passed by!

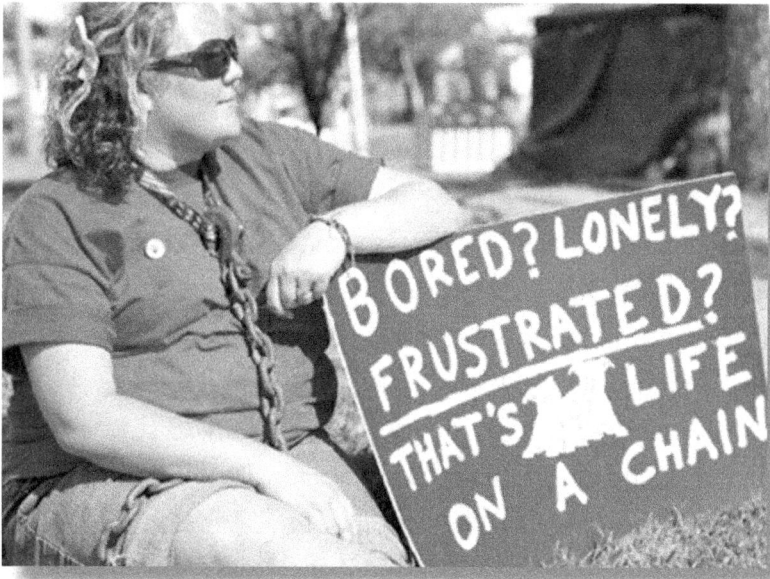

DDB Rep Amanda Green leads her volunteers in Albuquerque, New Mexico.

YEAR EIGHT: JUNE -JULY, 2011

⊗⊗

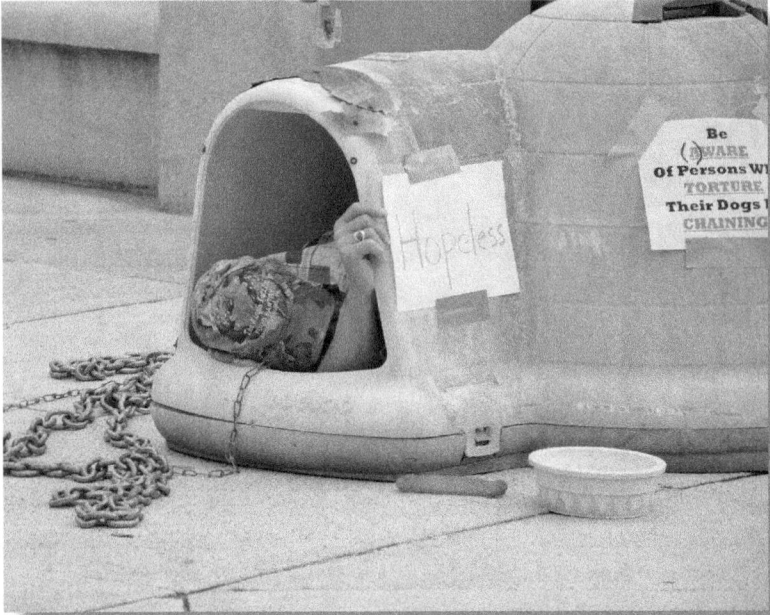

Gordon Bakalar put a lot of thought into his doghouse at the 2011 Chain Off in Pennsylvania. He made signs for passers-by to read, and curled up inside with his chain and empty bowl visually simulating the everyday life of a chained dog.

I've already shared with you the 2011 Pennsylvania State Capitol Chain Off, wherein we chained 40 people to doghouses, and at the end of the day rewarded them for good behavior with a Doghouse Wedding. Ha!

Nationally we ended up with 81 people in 18 states, including Arizona, California, Connecticut, Florida, Illinois, Iowa, Maryland, Michigan, Minnesota, Missouri, New Mexico, New York, Pennsylvania, Tennessee, Washington, West Virginia, Wisconsin, Wyoming, and Guam.

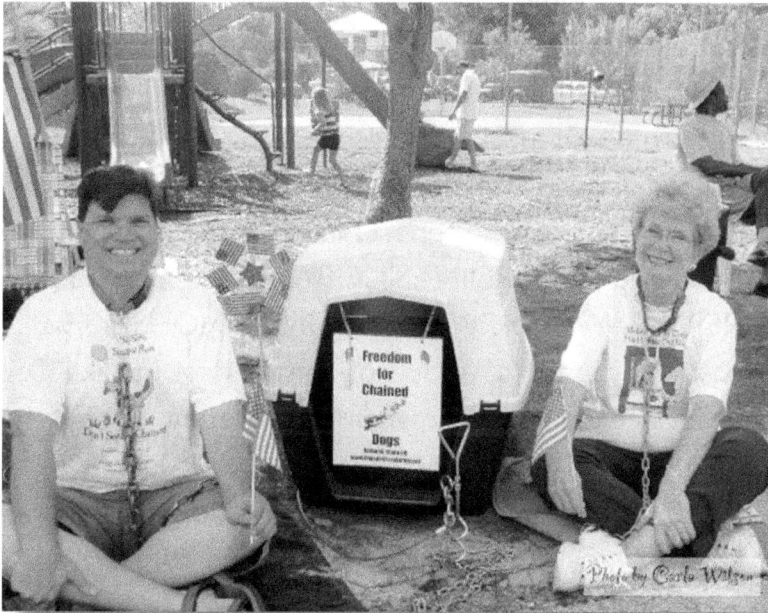

Bryan Wilson and Nancy McDavid in Groveland, Florida.

Nancy McDavid, Florida, told us: "We passed out brochures, and showed a photo album of 'My Life on a Chain,' featuring a two-year old dog near me who tragically succumbed to the heat in June of 2011. It was a stark reality for people to see the horrible neglect and cruelty these dogs have to endure. Many shook their heads in disbelief.

"It was encouraging to see so many people supportive of passing a law against the chaining of dogs. Quite a few visitors had stories of their own and wanted to know what they could do about it. The local newspapers printed an advance story about our Chain Off which drew people to the festival from the other side of the county—just to visit our booth."

As a side note to the Florida Chain Off, Nancy succeeded in getting her county law the next year! Here's the update I posted in our e-newsletter from March, 2012: "There were many times

Nancy McDavid almost lost her spark while fighting for a law in the past year, but many of us came along and cheered her on, and some joined her team locally. She was inspired to create chain-ge from watching her neighbor dog, Chomper, languish and finally die at the end of a chain. Enough was enough.

"Today we're happy to report Nancy has succeeded! She told us: 'We did it! AN ORDINANCE BANNING UNATTENDED TETHERING WAS APPROVED UNANIMOUSLY 5-0! The Commissioners "got it." Woo-hoo for the dogs in Lake County. The ordinance calls for the owner to be present when tethering their dog."

This, my friends, is further proof that one person on a mission can really make a difference for chained dogs.

YEAR NINE: JUNE -JULY, 2012

⊙⊙

By 2012 I was encouraging folks to take the Chain Off campaigns to their state Capitol buildings. I realized from my time at the Pennsylvania state Capitol that it wasn't THAT intimidating, AND if we wanted to change laws, we needed to get on the radar screens of senators and house reps with the power to back bills in committee.

Unfortunately, I also failed to remember that many citizens are scared (as I was) to go to their state Capitols even for lobby day—let alone to pull up a doghouse and chain and stay awhile! I couldn't blame them.

I ended up making a ten state Capitol Doghouse Tour that year, and along the way people met me and chained up with me at their state Capitol buildings. Other than my tour, the only people who took on their state Capitol were Melody Whitworth and Sheila Ehler—both DDB reps—in Missouri.

A few others did Chain Offs in parks and other public places like I'd done in the past, but we didn't have nearly the participation I had come to expect. I was disheartened.

I suspected it was like most things...it had its time, and then people moved on to something else. Another TV show, another movie series...it's just the way of the world.

Meanwhile, though, in backyards all across America, the dogs still waited for help that hadn't come. If Chain Off was to be a thing of the past, what campaign would take its place so that dogs have voices raised on their behalf? Good question.

All in all, that year we ended up with 45 participants and hit 16 states, including: Arizona, Colorado, Connecticut, Florida, Maryland, Massachusetts, Michigan, Missouri, New Hampshire, New Jersey, New York, North Carolina, Ohio, Pennsylvania, Rhode Island, Virginia, and Guam.

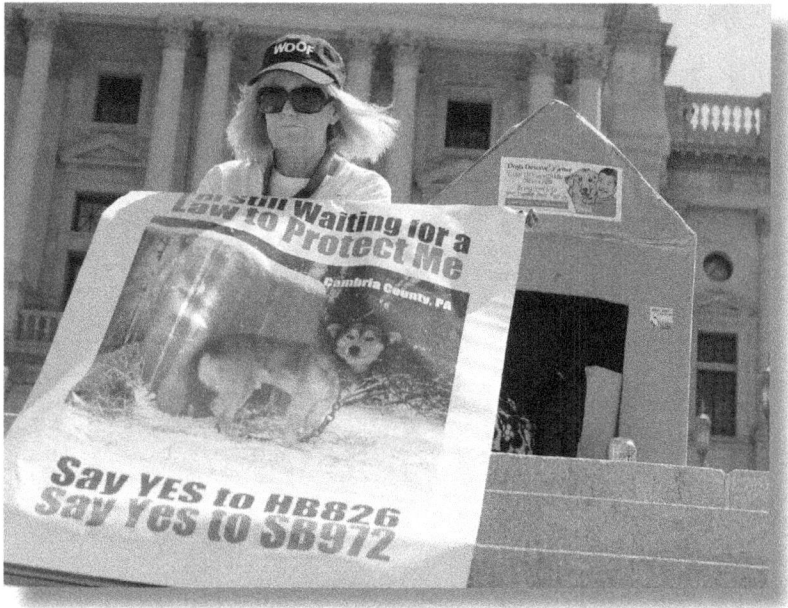

Janis Lindenberger puts in the time on a chain at the PA Capitol steps.

On the Ten State Tour, I started in Pennsylvania then worked me way around the Northeast, with New York being the last state of the year. I was so proud of the 11 supporters who came out in Pennsylvania that I wrote this in my blog: "I felt like a proud mamma hen out there. The ones who showed up came despite their fears. It takes courage to come out to the grandest building in the state—full of stuffed shirts and suits—and pull up a doghouse, then don a thick logging chain while people stare at you like you're nuts.

"We must remember that each and every movement in history started because people were willing to be perceived as crazy in doing something different to make a change. Eventually, with enough time and effort on the part of those who carried the passion, things changed for the better. This will too.

"Don't our dogs deserve for us to be a little nuts about them and for them? I'd say so."

Charay Malas (left) brought a stuffed dog to chain with us in New Hampshire.

There ended up being two legislative surprises on the tour that year. In Rhode Island I was there in a "Thank You" capacity, because legislators had just passed a law limiting chaining to 10 hours a day.

And then, in Delaware, I was asked NOT to chain up for the day by advocates because they were waiting on the governor to sign their bill into law. They feared that my presence might tick him off and cause him instead to refuse to sign; I didn't want or need that on my conscience. So I agreed not to chain up, which turned out to be fortuitous because the van broke down and I had to spend the day getting it fixed anyway.

Meanwhile, the Delaware bill passed and was signed into law!

In Boston, MaryBeth McCluskey simulated a dog suffering heat exhaustion.

YEAR TEN: JULY & NOVEMBER, 2013

In 2013 I was coming off a 30-day hunger strike in which I'd ended up hospitalized for two days; I was taking a stand against defamatory attacks on myself and Dogs Deserve Better by Surry County, Virginia authorities who wanted to rid themselves of our 'unwelcome presence' through lies and false arrests.

I wasn't in a good place mentally or physically to be doing an extensive Chain Off activist campaign, so I opted to simply do the Pennsylvania state Capitol and the Virginia state Capitol.

All told, that year we had 55 people standing up for chained dogs in Colorado, Maryland, Massachusetts, New Mexico, Pennsylvania, Virginia, and Washington.

Teens in Pennsylvania enjoyed making a difference and learning how activism works.

The New Mexico Chain Off was an interesting addition to the 2013 lineup; I flew out in November, in conjunction with Sunny Aris and her organization, Animal Village New Mexico, and she hosted an entire day-long festival for her event.

About 15 people came by and chained up with me, taking donations to get themselves off the chains; and—in the coolest turn of events yet—both a Sheriff and a Sheriff's Deputy took turns chaining up with us! For once, I was on the right side of the law! And, they agreed with us. Will miracles never cease.

Sheriff's Deputy Darren chained up in New Mexico.

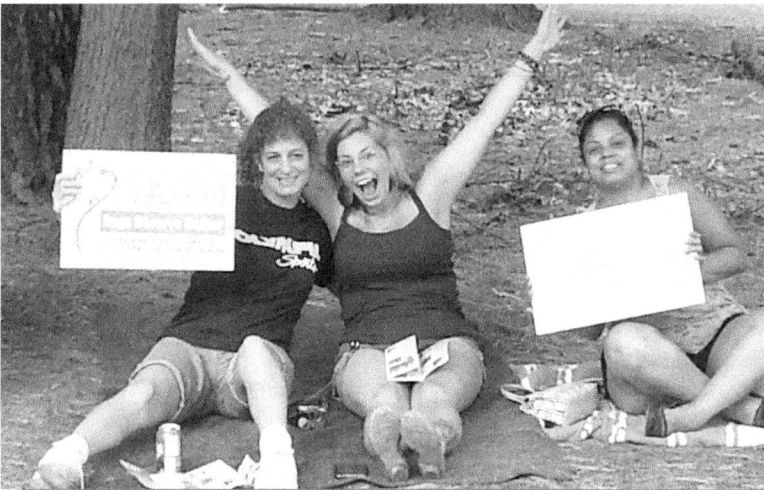

Volunteers in Massachusetts were super-excited to chain up for the dogs!

YEAR ELEVEN: JULY, 2014

๑๑

In 2014 I was back up to steam, undertaking a seven state Capitol Doghouse Tour, wherein I chained myself in front of state Capitols in West Virginia, Ohio, Indiana, Illinois, Missouri, Kentucky, and Virginia. I was able to directly reach decision-makers in each state by bringing the message to their doorstep, and along the way I was joined by 21 others who donned chains and/or held signs and educated the public.

In addition, dog advocates like Theresa Hearn in Colorado, Bryan Wilson in Florida, Kristina Jones in Maine, and Jean Gilbert in New Mexico joined us again that year and inspired others to come out with them. Others in New Mexico, New York, North Carolina, and Texas chained up too, for a total of 48 people nationwide.

Theresa Arguello-Hearn (right) and her team in Pueblo, Colorado.

One Pennsylvania advocate, Joe Maringo from SPARRO Rescue, remembered seeing me at my first local event way back in 2002, and thinking to himself "there's no way that will ever take off." But, for the 2014 Chain Off, Joe wore a broken collar and chain around town, educating everyone he spoke to along the way about the dangers of chaining.

That, folks, is the power of activism!

Joe Maringo wore a chain all day as he ran errands in Pennsylvania.

In Kentucky, I was joined by the volunteers at SOAR for my last day.

WILL THERE BE MORE CHAIN OFFS IN THE FUTURE?

☟☜

In 2015, I left the organization I founded, passing the reins to a new board and a new director. I'm saddened to say DDB has, as of this writing, not undertaken any Chain Offs or other new advocacy or activist programs for chained dogs.

They have contented themselves with rescuing dogs at the Good Newz Rehab Center, but little else.

I'm disheartened and heartbroken by this, because the chained dogs need strong voices, and Dogs Deserve Better's voice was not only the strongest, but the first to take the stand.

I wrote this short article about Chain Off in 2014, and my argument still stands today:

> *Dogs Deserve Better has rescued a lot of chained dogs, and we provide vet care grants for a lot more that are rescued by other groups too. We believe in the rescue world's favorite adage, "Rescuing one dog might not chain-ge the world, but the world will surely chain-ge for that one dog."*
>
> *There is no greater satisfaction for us than watching a dog who existed in his/her own filth and neglect come to life in the arms of our rescue.*
>
> *But, we recognize that DDB bears a large part of the burden for creating chain-ge around the issue of dog chaining, and the nation and world will be slow to evolve if we stick solely to rescue and ignore other avenues such as education, legislation, and activism. These avenues are mission-essential and create a bigger impact on ALL dogs stuck out at the end of a chain, not just the relatively few we are able to rescue,*

rehabilitate, and rehome into loving families.

Our largest activist campaign—Chain Off—rolls out every June-July, and raises awareness for chained dogs by the simple act of picking up a collar and chain, placing them around our necks, and putting ourselves in the dogs' paws for the world to see.

Most people are unaware that it's still legal in most areas of the U.S. to chain a dog for life, and they are appalled when they find out it's still going on. Often, citizens are inspired by our actions to talk to state reps or local city councils in order to create better legislation that protects the dogs from this abuse. By donning a chain, we stand up for the rights of those who have none.

It is my heartfelt opinion that Dogs Deserve Better and we as citizens who care about the plight of the chained dog must continue to be active on their behalf. There is no other way to win them the freedom they so justly deserve.

By the end of 2014, I had spent 877 hours chained to a dog-house. 877 hours! Yet that pales in comparison to the amount of time most chained dogs will spend in their lives. It's a sobering thought.

In closing, I'd like to share with you a free-form piece I wrote for the dogs, also from my last year doing Chain Off. It's not my 'usual style,' but I liked it, and it was passionately written.

As further food for thought, I am more than willing to partici-pate in and/or lead Chain Offs again in the future under the aus-pices of another nonprofit. Any group that would like to hold one, please contact me through my publishing company at who-chainsyou.com to plan accordingly.

Thank you for reading, and thank you for taking action on the dogs' behalf. They need you, they need ALL OF US to speak up for them.

It's Too Long
on Too Short Chains

AND WE'RE TOO QUIET

⚭

by Tamira Thayne

I'm looking at a black dog on a chain and it's too long to spend your life and the chain is too short to spend your days and I've been **too quiet for too long.**

I take a stand even if that stand is alone and it doesn't matter if it's alone because it's been too long.

It's 2002 and it's been hundreds of years and there's no one

no one

no one

to help them and everyone throws up their hands everyday that "it's not my problem" and "it's just the way it is" and "there's nothing we can do" about it.

So I strap a chain a thick chain a **logging chain around my neck** with a dog collar and I pull up some pantyhose and a black skirt and **I sit I stand I sleep I lay at the end of that chain for 1 day and 9 hours for 33 hours for 1980 minutes.** It's 2004.

The next year I do it again because it's still too long the sickness is still too deep the hell is still too real and the solutions are still too so not enough.

And you join me.

You join me as few, you join me as many, you join me because **for you too it's been too long on too short chains and you too know we're too quiet.**

100 of you join me with chains and doghouses and **faces of victory over your own fears** and years go by and I'm grateful that I'm not alone I'm so grateful and yet it's not enough it's never enough because they are

STILL.

THERE.

We collectively decide we may not be enough we are never enough so we

STOP

TRYING.

Where I envision 100 dog-loving humans then 1000 dog-loving humans then 10,000 dog-loving humans who **insist no demand no REQUIRE that humans stop chaining our best friends**, we become

50 and then 40 and

then 4.

Is the shame the embarrassment the ridicule of standing on a chain for a dog who stands on a chain

with no voice in his government

no words in his mouth

no thoughts in his skull

except

HELP

ME

too much?

I wonder

am I too radical too crazy too over the top or am I too scared too withdrawn too timid to be what inspires you to **do battle for dogs with voices chained by abusive humans.**

I don't know I can't know I will never know.

I know that it's 2014 and It's still Too Long on Too Short Chains and We're still Too Quiet.

I know we can't quit we can't stop we can't abandon them.

If I were the magic that inspires I would bring our government 100,000 chained humans who love dogs to say no more no more no more

NEVER

AGAIN.

If I were the magic that galvanizes I would fire the greatest the largest the grandest revolution for dogs by humans and we would stand as one with one voice and one requirement:

that dogs would be loved as ourselves.

If I were the magic

the magic

the magic

Dogs would be FREE.

Acknowledgments

When I was pregnant with my son Rayne (but didn't know it yet), an astrologer I told me never to have kids on my own because I couldn't handle it.

Yet I somehow managed to parent two kids (it remains to be seen how well), 250 furkids, and 'parented' DDB to its pre-teen years, which has been the biggest challenge of my life.

I could never have brought the org and this book to fruition were it not for the work, help, and support of so, so many people of like mind, many of whom go unsung and unmentioned.

For this campaign my biggest thanks go to Joe, for being there for me absolutely every minute he could and always believing in me; I never knew what that was like before you. To Mike Romberger, who willingly took on the job of campaign manager, coordinating doghouse runs and multiple other tasks, not to mention the kick-ass article he wrote which is printed herein; and to Mark Shaffer who faithfully showed up most mornings to help me set up the doghouse so I didn't have to wheel it down on my own.

I thank all of you who supported me, chained in my stead, and sent letters and donated to the campaign. I'm so, so grateful.

For spreading the word and the work for chained dogs with enthusiasm and diligence, I thank the hundreds who donned collars and chains and suffered humiliation to become a voice for the voiceless. I have thousands of photos of you wonderfully-humane humans, and if your photo wasn't pictured or you were not mentioned by name, know that I'm still grateful to you for every minute you put into the cause. Never doubt that.

I hope you'll continue to support the chained dogs and the organizations who work on their behalf. They deserve our best, and we must strive to give them our all at all times.

To the dogs!

About the Author

Tamira Thayne pioneered the anti-tethering movement in America, forming and leading the nonprofit Dogs Deserve Better for 13 years. During her time on the front lines of animal activism and rescue she took on plenty of bad guys (often failing miserably); her swan song culminated in the purchase and transformation of Michael Vick's dogfighting compound to a chained-dog rescue and rehabilitation center.

Tamira's spent 878 hours chained to a doghouse on behalf of the voiceless in front of state capitol buildings nationwide; her organization rescued and rehabilitated thousands of chained dogs, finding them new, inside homes and families.

In 2016 she founded Who Chains You, publishing books by and for animal activists and rescuers. Tamira is the author of *The Wrath of Dog, The King's Tether, Foster Doggie Insanity,* and *Capitol in Chains,* and the co-editor of *Unchain My Heart* and *Rescue Smiles.*

www.ingramcontent.com/pod-product-compliance
Lightning Source LLC
LaVergne TN
LVHW051622080426
835511LV00016B/2129